ARE YOU DOING TH

CUTTING

BINGEING

SNORTING

INTERNET

ALCOHOL

SPORTING

Renée C. Rebman

Originally published as *Addictions and Risky Behaviors: Cutting, Bingeing, Snorting, and Other Dangers* in 2006.

No part of this book may be reproduced by any means without the written permission of the publisher.

Library of Congress Cataloging-in-Publication Data

Rebman, Renée C., 1961–
  [Addictions and risky behaviors]
  Are you doing risky things? : cutting, bingeing, snorting, and other dangers / Renée C. Rebman.
pages cm. — (Got issues?)
  Includes bibliographical references and index.
  Summary: "Find out about a number of addictions: drugs, alcohol, inhalant abuse, smoking, eating disorders, self-mutilation, and the Internet"—Provided by publisher.
  ISBN 978-0-7660-5996-2
  1. Substance abuse—Juvenile literature. 2. Compulsive behavior—Juvenile literature. 3. Risk- taking (Psychology)—Juvenile literature. I. Title.
  HV4998.R43 2014 613.8—dc23

                                                2013010618

Future Editions:
Paperback ISBN: 978-0-7660-5997-9
EPUB ISBN: 978-0-7660-5998-6
Single-User PDF ISBN: 978-0-7660-5999-3
Mulit-User PDF ISBN: 978-0-7660-6031-9

Printed in the United States of America

062014 Lake Book Manufacturing, Inc., Melrose Park, IL

10 9 8 7 6 5 4 3 2 1

To Our Readers: We have done our best to make sure that all Internet Addresses in this book were active and appropriate when we went to press. However, the author and publisher have no control over and assume no liability for the material available on those Internet sites or on other Web sites they may link to. Any comments or suggestions can be sent by e-mail to comments@enslow.com or to the address on the back cover.

♻ Enslow Publishers, Inc., is committed to printing our books on recycled paper. The paper in every book contains 10% to 30% post-consumer waste (PCW). The cover board on the outside of each book contains 100% PCW. Our goal is to do our part to help young people and the environment too!

Illustration Credits: Centers for Disease Control and Prevention, p. 39; iStockphoto (MachineHeadz, p. 58; mandygodbehear, p. 89); Shutterstock.com (© aceshot1, p. 67; ©antoshkaforever, p. 14; © Artem © Furman, p. 64; © aslysun, p. 1; © CREATISTA, p. 8; © Doreen Salcher, p. 46; © dwphotos, p. 16; © gh19, p. 35;© iofoto, p. 25; J © John Panella, p. 28; © jstudio, p. 61; © LaCameraChiara, p. 5; © Mariusz Szachowski, p. 43; © Mehmet Dilsiz, p. 12; © OLJ Studio, p. 53; © Tan Kian Khoon, p. 32; © wong yu liang, p. 73); © Thinkstock (James Pauls, p. 82; Jupiterimages, p. 86; Stockbyte, p. 76); Tobacco Control Research Branch of the National Cancer Institute, p. 49.

Cover Illustrations: Shutterstock.com/ © aslysun

Contents

For my brother, Jerry R. Zajack, Jr.

The Addiction Risk

Addictions come in many forms. Some, such as an addiction to alcohol or drugs, have a direct physical impact or chemical change to the body. Other addictions, such as eating disorders, are in the form of a risky behavior or dangerous habit. Addictions can be characterized by what they have in common.

An addicted person has a heightened need or severe craving for whatever his or her particular addiction is. When denied access to it, the addict will suffer from withdrawal. He or she may feel actual physical pain, discomfort, or an uncontrollable feeling of anxiety. Addicts show a willingness to give up other things in order to indulge in their addiction—sometimes to the point of self-destruction. They may lose family, friends, or even their jobs during their quest to satisfy their addiction.

Some addicts fall victim to more than one type of addiction. For example, an anorexic may also engage in self-mutilation; an alcoholic may also have a problem with drugs.

Addictions can rip apart families and sometimes even cause death. Teen addictions are especially painful. Young people often do not ask for, or even want, the help they need. Parents are caught unaware and unprepared to deal with the problem. If families are fortunate, the addiction is discovered in time. But the heartbreak and pain of discovery and rehabilitation is unavoidable. In less fortunate cases, the outcome can be devastating.

Damien Massella, a seventeen-year-old high school graduate, had plans to attend culinary school at a local community college. But Damien was addicted to alcohol and drugs. He spent a night partying in the woods with his friends. He never made it home. His body was found slumped against a tree. He had died from a heroin overdose.[1]

His parents established "Damien's Run For Recovery," a five-kilometer run and two-mile walk to raise money for teenagers recovering from addictions. Gina, Damien's mother, hopes to raise not only money, but also awareness. She said, "Addiction is a problem nobody wants to talk about, but hopefully this race can make people more aware of the problem."[2]

Rick Marion, one of Damien's high school friends who volunteered at the race, says, "It's a great cause. After what happened to Damien, this is a problem that I take very seriously because it cost me one of my good friends."[3]

Unfortunately, many teens like Damien experiment with drugs and run the risk of becoming addicted. But why?

Changes and Pressures

The answer to the question "why?" is complicated. Teenage years are stressful. Young people are forced to deal with added responsibilities and more difficult classes at school. At the same time, they are dealing with their changing bodies as they go through puberty. Their friends may also exert peer pressure to try new things. Teenagers are thrust into a world full of temptation, a world in which they desperately want to fit in.

Teens sometimes turn to drugs to impress their friends, to rebel against authority, or as a means of escaping anxiety or depression. They may begin using drugs as a response to popular culture or messages they see and hear in the media.[4] They mistakenly believe that "everyone is doing it" and that drugs, smoking, and other addictive behaviors are "cool." Recent surveys indicate that 54 percent of teens will try an illicit drug before they leave high school.[5]

Rick and Chris Hillesheim are a couple raising three boys. They strongly believe the pressures of society make it tough for teens to make good choices. They find modern culture full of negative images and messages.

"They are bombarded with far more than we ever were. They are bombarded on all sides: TV, music, peer pressure," Mrs. Hillesheim says. "It has forced kids to make moral judgments in an almost amoral society."[6]

They feel it is important to keep their sons busy and show them plenty of support. The Hillesheims have gotten their boys involved in after-school activities such as sports and music to teach them discipline and give them something positive to do. They also believe that religious faith has helped instill morals in their sons and kept them grounded.[7]

Not Just Drugs

Drugs may be the most obvious dangerous addiction teens face, but there are others. Eating disorders are frightening and on the rise. Anorexia (restricting one's eating to the point of malnutrition and excessive weight loss) and bulimia (bingeing on food and then inducing vomiting) are conditions experienced by many teens who attempt to gain a false sense of control over their bodies, meanwhile causing physical and mental damage.

Teen addictions can tear a family apart.

Becky is a teenager suffering from anorexia. Her obsessive fear of gaining weight, losing control, and not being perfect led her to restrict her diet to a severe degree. Her typical daily intake included a breakfast of tea and dry toast, a lunch of one apple and two rice cakes, a salad for dinner, and a chocolate drink for a snack.

Becky's anxiety over food and calories was overwhelming. She entered therapy to get help. During her sessions she admitted that she was also bulimic: "I never, ever, eat anything without throwing up."[8]

Becky lives in fear of gaining weight. Like most anorexics, she cannot stop her behavior. During her therapy sessions she admitted how scary it was for her to try to put on weight. The rituals and strict rules she had set for herself had taken over her life.

Brenda, a sixteen-year-old anorexic, said she feels that her anorexia, and the ensuing weight loss, brought her admiration from her peers. Her comments show how desperate she is to cling to her behavior regardless of how it might affect her health:

I love that all my friends tell me how great I look since I lost weight. They all want to know how I did it. I never tell them, of course. Now, I feel as though I could never gain the weight back, not anymore, then I will lose all this respect.[9]

Another dangerous behavior practiced by teenagers is known as self-mutilation. This most commonly means cutting one's own skin, though it can involve burning, biting, or other types of self-injury. Those who practice cutting claim that it gives them an emotional release. Current statistics show that this behavior is on the rise and is found in all social and economic groups.

A study conducted in one large urban Massachusetts high school found that 3 percent (sixty out of eighteen hundred students) were self-mutilators. Many of these kids were not perceived to be at-risk or problem students. Barent Walsh, PhD, spoke at a conference on self-destructive behaviors sponsored by Harvard Medical School and explained the results of the study: "[Self-mutilators] were not in special education; many had good grades and were socially connected."[10] He went on to say the behavior was possibly connected to self-loathing or perceived failure, and that it provided a "powerful communication" to attract the attention of unresponsive people.[11] In other words, their actions may be a cry for help.

On-line Addiction

Addictive behaviors do not simply include those that target the body; they also include those that isolate teenagers and keep them from enjoying normal life. Addiction to the Internet is one example. Many teens spend countless hours immersed in chat rooms or playing interactive games. This obsession is compared to pathological gambling or compulsive shopping. In 1997, the American Psychological Association officially recognized Internet addiction as a mental health disorder.[12]

While it is difficult to determine what constitutes excessive on-line time, sometimes the answer is evident. Daniel Rivero, age fifteen, offers his opinion on the problem, "I don't think it's healthy to use the Internet as a substitute for reality. It's OK to go on-line for entertainment reasons, but it's not OK if that's what most of your life consists of."[13]

Errol Parsons, also age fifteen, agrees, "I think when the Internet starts to affect your grades and affect your social life then you have gone too far."[14]

In some instances social media has taken the place of actual interaction. Many teens spend hours on the popular Facebook site contacting hundreds of "friends" they may have actually never met.

With the popularity and, some would say, the necessity of being on-line rising, this issue is sure to be debated for some time. Meanwhile, many teens are being lost to an alternate reality in cyberspace.

Instant access to others is also available through texting by cell phone. Some teens send dozens of quick messages to others at all times of the day and night. While seemingly harmless, this activity has proven deadly as many teens text while driving. Cell phones have also presented the problem of sexting; with teens sending explicit messages and pictures. This behavior is so widespread that seventeen states have enacted laws to address youth sexting and another thirteen states have legislation pending.[15]

Are all teens at risk for addiction of some kind? The temptation is there, and the opportunity for risky behavior is probably present for almost every teen, but addiction need not be a foregone conclusion. Understanding the risks and learning ways to cope with problems, avoid trouble, and how to get help when needed can keep addictive behavior out of a teen's lifestyle.

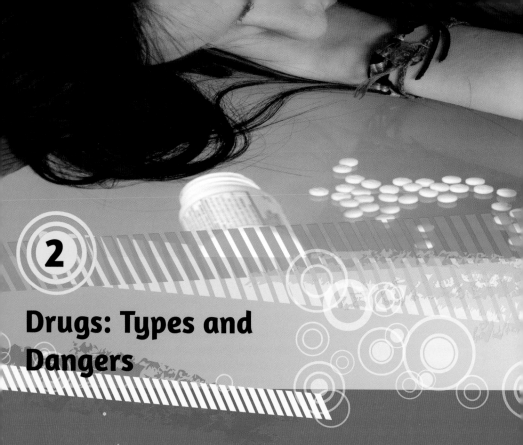

2

Drugs: Types and Dangers

When considering addictions, illicit drugs are often the first substance that comes to mind. Some studies indicate that drug use among teenagers is down, but drugs are still a clear danger to adolescents. Many teens experiment with drugs thinking it will not become a problem for them—that they will not become addicted. But there are real-life stories that show these assumptions are sometimes wrong.

Laura was seventeen when her experimentation with drugs began. At first she tried ecstasy and "absolutely loved it."[1] But the good feelings did not last. The next time she tried it, she broke out in a cold sweat.

Laura looked for another high. She ended up switching to heroin and became hooked. She had to turn to shoplifting to support her drug habit. Laura was eventually arrested and ended up at Phoenix House, a drug rehabilitation center. She got off drugs and pieced her life back together. But she has a warning for others concerning the dangers of the drug that got her started: "Ecstasy can cause heart problems and brain damage. It's not worth it for the three hours of feeling happy."[2]

Many Names, Many Dangers

Some of the most commonly abused drugs have various street names and come in different forms. They also can be used in different ways and have many, sometimes serious, effects on the body. The following short list covers just a few of the most abused drugs.

Cocaine: This is a white or yellow powder that is injected or inhaled. It increases breathing, heart rate, and body temperature. Users may experience insomnia, loss of appetite, and seizures. Cocaine can cause death by cardiac arrest or respiratory failure. Crack cocaine has the same hazards. It comes in the form of white or tan pellets and is most often smoked.[3]

Methamphetamines: This substance is usually referred to as crystal meth. It comes in the form of powder, pills, or rocks and is taken orally, injected, or inhaled. Crystal meth increases heart rate, breathing, and body temperature.[4]

LSD: This hallucinogen is taken orally, either by tablets, powder, liquids, or blotter paper. LSD causes hallucinations and distorted perceptions.[5]

Marijuana: This drug consists of dried leaves, stems, and seeds that are coarser than tobacco. It can be smoked or taken orally. Marijuana causes impaired perceptions, difficulty in concentration, increased appetite, and lack of motivation.[6]

Reasons for Drug Use

Why teens use drugs is a topic that is often debated. There are many reasons drugs have become a part of teen culture. Reaction to peer pressure is one such reason. Drugs may make a teen feel important,

cocaine—coke, snow, blow, toot, sneeze

crack cocaine—crack, rock, freebase, blue

heroin—horse, glass, gravy, H

LSD—acid, microdot, blotter acid, flash

marijuana—pot, reefer, grass, weed, dope, ganja, mary jane

methamphetamines—crystal meth, bling bling, fast

steroids—gym candy, pumpers

inhalants—poppers, kick, bang, huff

bath salts—vanilla sky, cloud nine, hurricane charlie, ivory wave

Spice—K2, genie, black mamba, fake weed

grown up, and give them a sense of status among their friends. Drugs may give them acceptance among some peer groups. Drugs also produce a welcome, though temporary "high"—a feeling of euphoria or well-being.

Using drugs may symbolize rebellion. It can also be a means to escape problems or used as recreation. Teens find it exciting to do something their parents or other authority figures would not approve of, something forbidden.[7]

How Many Are at Risk?

How many teens are actively using drugs? It appears the number is on the decline. A recent survey found that for the first time ever, more than half of American teenagers say their schools are drug free. Columbia University's National Survey of American Attitudes on Substance Abuse said that 62 percent reported they did not see drugs kept, used, or sold at school in 2002, up from 42 percent in 2000, and up from a low of 31 percent in 1988.[8]

One ninth-grade teacher at North Miami Beach Senior High School in Florida was unimpressed by the survey, saying, "That study must not have been from Miami because some of my students sell drugs right from my classroom."[9] It seems probable that this sentiment could be echoed in classrooms around the country. The war on drugs is not won yet.

Ecstasy: A Hazardous Trend

While some drug use has declined, use of other drugs has increased. Ecstasy is becoming one of the most popular fad drugs, and its usage among teens increased by 20 percent from 2000 to 2001.[10] Studies estimate about 2.9 million teens had experimented with it at that time.[11]

Ecstasy works by releasing large amounts of serotonin, a neurotransmitter, in the brain. This release causes feelings of well-being, love, and acceptance and has earned ecstasy the nickname

Ecstasy has become one of the most popular party drugs among teens. Its use can cause addictions and severe medical problems.

the "hug drug."[12] Users report experiencing feelings of extreme euphoria.

Logan Corcoran started using ecstasy at the age of fourteen when she began going to dance parties. Every Saturday night Logan would get high. She loved the way ecstasy made her feel:

"There's no way you can describe how it affects you. It's like every sense is magnified 500 times, and everything seems so real. It's illogical that even a Snapple bottle can be so beautiful and profound and perfect. But that's the way it makes you feel."[13]

Under the influence of ecstasy, Logan never felt afraid. She said, "Someone can pull a gun on you, and you wouldn't even be scared."[14]

Her addiction was taking over her life. She sought treatment but kept returning to her old habits. "I'd think I'd be doing really good. I'd say, 'I'll just do a little bit of ecstasy or coke or acid,'" she said. "But prom night 1999, I went nuts."[15]

That night Logan and her date combined ecstasy with LSD. She has no memory of what happened after she took the drugs. Somehow, she got home and found herself on the floor, begging her parents for help.

"Using ecstasy can make you feel good, like you fit in and like everyone in the world is your friend," says Erin Artigiani, director of the Center for Substance Abuse. "But it's an artificial high, and it won't last. Teenagers have to be educated about all of this."[16]

Parents also need to be aware. And many parents, although they know about ecstasy, refuse to believe their children would ever try it. A reported 12 percent of seventh through twelfth graders have used the drug at least once. Steve Pasierb, president of the Partnership for a Drug-Free America, is disturbed by the gap between facts and adult perception of the problem. "The level of denial is pretty drastic here," he says.[17]

Raves

Like many others, Logan began her drug use while attending raves. Raves are all-night dance parties attended by hundreds of people, usually between the ages of fourteen to thirty. Unlike legitimate clubs, raves are often unlicensed, identification is not required, and underage partygoers are admitted with no restrictions. Many times, the actual address of the party is not revealed until the last minute; locations can change often and quickly. Some raves may be in a certain location for one night only.

Raves are characterized by loud, deafening music, smoke machines, laser lights, and the drug dealing that goes on, often out in the open. The proportion of teens actually using drugs at raves is difficult to determine; anywhere from 10 to 90 percent has been estimated.[18]

Sergeant Michael Lemon of the Detroit Police narcotics division has a strong opinion of raves. "It's just a dope party with music," he says.[19]

The dancers who take drugs in the overcrowded, broiling-hot raves face a very real risk of becoming dehydrated as their body temperatures rise to dangerous levels. Their kidneys can fail, and they can experience seizures. Many teens have been sent to emergency centers after attending raves.

Marijuana

Marijuana has been a tremendously controversial drug for decades. Many people support its legalization, at least for medicinal purposes. Marijuana has many positive uses. It is used to treat AIDS symptoms, reduce nausea, reduce eye pressure in glaucoma patients, and control muscle spasms associated with epilepsy and multiple sclerosis.[20]

Opponents of legalization argue that lack of tight controls would make monitoring dosages impossible. They believe that some patients who seek medicinal marijuana may in fact be habitual users simply looking for easy access to the drug.[21] Those who support medicinal use argue that restrictions would be effective in controlling marijuana use. Doctors' prescriptions would be necessary to obtain the drug, and the medical community would monitor which patients needed and would have access to marijuana.

There are also some people who feel that marijuana should be made legal for everyone's use. They claim that it is no more harmful than alcohol and should be available for everyone of legal age.

Research indicates that among users, marijuana use usually begins around age thirteen and a half.[22] Current studies show that recreational use of marijuana can be more dangerous than some believe. John Walters, director of the Office of National Drug Control Policy, says many parents and teens have outdated perceptions about the drug, believing it to be nonaddictive and less dangerous than cigarettes.

"Our effort is to correct the ignorance that is the single biggest obstacle to protecting our kids."[23] Walters also points out that more teens enter rehabilitation centers to treat marijuana addiction than alcohol or all illegal drugs combined.[24]

Research shows that not only can marijuana be addictive, but it is also more potent than the marijuana of past decades. It directly affects the brain, impairing the ability of young people to concentrate and retain information during their peak learning years. It also weakens short-term memory and interferes with the brain mechanisms that form long-term memory.[25]

The obvious dangers of the drug to the body are not the only concern. Thousands of tragic automobile accidents are linked to drivers operating under the influence of marijuana. In such instances, recreational use is more than dangerous—it can prove fatal.

Have the dangers of marijuana been downplayed in recent years? Is it a gateway to harder drugs? Should the drug be legalized? The controversy is bound to continue.

Designer Drugs

A dangerous new trend teens are involved with is designer drugs. These drugs are manufactured with synthetic chemicals which are added to various substances in such a way as to avoid federal regulations. Because their chemical makeup narrowly escapes being illegal, these substances are readily available in smoke shops, and even convenience stores. They are relatively inexpensive and are presented in colorful packaging. Two of the most common are bath salts and spice.

Bath salts are not a relaxing beauty product. They are a white crystalline powder sold in small packets that can be smoked, snorted, or ingested to produce a dangerous high. It is a powerful hallucinogenic that can cause users to be aggressive and paranoid. Bath salts can also accelerate the heart rate, produce seizures, and even cause death. [26]

One bath salt tragedy occurred in Louisiana. A boy snorted the substance and spent days experiencing psychotic episodes before ultimately committing suicide. [27]

In the state of Washington, investigators determined that Army Sgt. David Stewart was using bath salts when he killed himself, his wife, and his five-year-old son.[28] Instances like these are causing many states to ban bath salts.

Spice, synthetic marijuana also known as K2, is another dangerous substance. It is a mixture of plant leaves and stems laced with chemicals and is smoked or even brewed into tea. In Illinois, a teenager died after smoking synthetic marijuana when he drove his car into a house. He crashed into the bedroom of a toddler who was fortunately playing in the backyard at the time and escaped injury.[29] In South Carolina, an Anderson University basketball player experienced cramps and vision problems and died after using K2. [30]

While statistics show use of designer drugs is on the rise, communities are fighting back with bans and awareness programs.

Steroids

Steroids are a type of drug some athletes turn to hoping to gain strength and size and improvement in their performance. This trend has had some tragic consequences. As of 2002, steroids had been blamed for eighty deaths nationwide.[31]

The steroids taken by athletes are anabolic-androgenic steroids, usually just called anabolic steroids. (Anabolic refers to increasing muscle mass; androgenic refers to increasing masculine characteristics.) They should not be confused with corticosteroids, strong medications that reduce swelling and inflammation. Corticosteroids are used to treat such conditions as asthma and arthritis.

Anabolic steroids taken by athletes are synthetic (man-made) drugs derived from the male hormone testosterone. It is estimated that 10 to 20 percent of male high school athletes, up to 30 percent of college and professional athletes, and up to 80 percent of bodybuilders use steroids. The drugs are taken orally or injected; they are also known as roids, juice, or sauce. They increase body weight, strength, and endurance.

The possible side effects of anabolic steroids include an increase in appetite, an increase in energy, and trouble sleeping. Some people may also feel sad or irritable. Other side effects are more serious: Steroids can cause cardiovascular disease, liver tumors, jaundice (yellowing of the skin), fluid retention, high blood pressure, severe acne, and trembling. Men can experience sterility and baldness. Women may have growth of facial hair and a deeper voice. In adolescents, the drug can permanently stop bones from growing, resulting in shortened height for life. Users may also become aggressive or may experience paranoia, delusion, and impaired judgment. As testing for steroids has become more strict, some athletes have found ways to obtain human growth hormone (HGH), which poses many of the same risks.

Supplements

Other popular substances designed to improve appearance and strength include androstenedione, DHEA, GHB, creatine, and ephedra. These are known as supplements, and they differ from steroids because they lack some of the enzymes that steroids contain. But taking supplements is risky.

When athletes use supplements right before a game, it is known as "juicing." Juicing provides a quick boost of energy that raises the heart rate and metabolism. It can be fatal, especially during the heat and exertion of a strenuous game or practice. Yet many athletes feel the quick energy is worth the risk. Iris Shaffner of Blue Cross and Blue Shield's Healthy Competition Foundation calls the use of supplements "a growing public-health crisis."[32]

Shaffner and others point out the serious lack of regulations over supplement makers. Problems such as false labeling—including not listing some things that are in the product or even listing wrong dosage amounts—have been discovered. Supplements, unlike drugs, are not required to be safety tested before going to market. The Food and Drug Administration has been slow to establish minimum standards for quality.[33]

Recently, some supplements, particularly androstenedione and ephedra, have been the subject of federal, state, and local legislation and have been banned. Many professional athletic associations already banned ephedra use even before the federal ban. Lawsuits are being filed by people who have experienced physical problems after using ephedra. Despite legislation and lawsuits, a quick Internet search shows that the product and so-called "substitutes" are still available.

Girls at Risk

Health authorities point out that girls are using supplements and steroids in sharply increasing numbers. Hoping to maintain a lean but muscular look, young women expose themselves to the same serious health risks as males, with the added potential of destroying their ability to bear children.

One nineteen-year-old woman used steroids to obtain a perfect body and ended up disfiguring herself and risking her life. Obsessed with winning her first bodybuilding competition, she lifted weights and ate a high-protein diet. Then she drastically reduced her food and water intake while taking steroids and a diuretic (a substance that causes an increase in the amount of urine the kidneys produce). This was an attempt to build muscle and drain her body of fluid to make the muscle stand out. Her plan worked, and she won the competition.

But then she began eating and drinking normally again. Her weight shot up by twenty-five pounds in only three days. Her muscles pushed out to their full overdeveloped size and crushed blood vessels in her legs. She was in serious danger.

Surgeons had to cut open both legs to relieve pressure on her vascular system and remove significant amounts of the muscle tissue she had built.[34]

Dr. Charles E. Yesalis, a steroid authority at Pennsylvania State University, summed up his feelings on the dangers of steroids: "Unless young people are taught to know where and how to draw the line, to know that it's not right to try and win at all costs, they're not going to listen when you tell them steroids put their lives at risk for the glory of winning."[35]

Getting Clean

Misuse and abuse of drugs is part of the reality of our society. Choosing to stop using drugs may seem hard. Actually kicking the habit and getting clean is much more difficult. Professional therapy can help. But addicts do not always want or seek therapy. And sometimes an addiction is not readily apparent—either to the addict or to others. Teens with addictions may maintain good grades and their behavior may remain essentially unchanged. Parents may not know help is needed until a serious situation arises. One therapist relates his personal experience:

> *I have seen teens in my practice that are high-functioning in grades and school activities, and they are fairly compliant with home rules. They have gotten into scary situations on weekends with alcohol or drugs, however, and they pass out or are in accidents where everyone in the car was high or drunk. They get referred to me, and I sometimes find out they have serious substance abuse problems.*[36]

Even after therapy begins, there are no guarantees the treatment will keep the addict on track. One persuasive teen convinced his therapist to encourage his parents to be more lenient. His mother lives with guilt over the outcome of her decision to yield to the therapist's advice. She says:

> We know now that he really manipulated the therapist, but at the time we went along with this and gave our son more freedom. One night he went out with friends and had a really bad trip on LSD. He hasn't been the same since, and it has been years.[37]

Teens in treatment are urged to share their feelings. What this often reveals is a pattern of denial and rationalization. Addicts place the blame on others, usually their parents or other authority figures. One teen decided getting high was a well-deserved reward for living with a "bad" mother. After he got clean, the truth came out:

> My mom was on my case all the time, so I needed to get high with my friends just to get away from her. Of course I didn't want to admit to myself that she had a right to be on my case because of all the trouble I was in. I persuaded myself that I deserved to get high because she was such a witch.[38]

Ultimately, rationalization and denial solve nothing. And this behavior is not exclusive to teens. Some parents are just as reluctant to admit there is an addiction problem in the family.

Alcohol: The Drug of Choice

3

Alcoholism among teens is a serious problem. Alcohol is often a teen's drug of choice. Many teens begin drinking on impulse or because they find themselves in a situation where alcohol is being used and they want to fit in. They do not believe that their drinking will escalate or become a problem. In fact, MADD (Mothers Against Drunk Driving, a group dedicated to alcohol awareness for young people) reports that half of the nation's junior and senior high school students drink at least monthly.[1]

One reason this is a significant statistic is that teens can become addicted much more quickly than adults. A therapist at the Community Psychiatric Center Hospital in Santa Ana, California, found that it takes an adult from one to five years to become an alcoholic, but a teen can become one within six to eighteen months of heavy drinking.[2]

The amount of alcohol a person consumes is a deciding factor in the effect it has. Alcohol in small doses can have some positive effects. For example, it has been known for years that moderate alcohol consumption (such as one glass of wine a day) reduces the risk of heart disease and circulatory diseases. Recent Japanese research also indicates that moderate drinkers do better on IQ tests than nondrinkers—possibly because alcohol improves blood flow to the brain, enhancing memory and mental function.[3]

But too much alcohol has immediate and potentially dangerous effects. It is absorbed into the bloodstream in as little as five to ten minutes. When people drink too much, they can experience slurred speech and loss of coordination. More excessive consumption can result in staggering, double vision, loss of balance, nausea, vomiting, or even blindness and unconsciousness. Over time, heavy drinking is associated with coronary heart disease, cirrhosis of the liver, and cancer of the mouth, pharynx, larynx, esophagus, and liver.[4]

Drinking and Driving

One of the most serious problems the nation faces is drinking and driving. MADD reports that car crashes involving alcohol are the leading cause of death for young people age fifteen to twenty. Their statistics also show that 16,654 people were killed in alcohol-related crashes in 2004. This accounted for a staggering 39 percent of the 42,800 people killed in all automobile accidents nationwide.[5]

Prom time is especially dangerous. In 1999, MADD estimates, more than one thousand people across the country died because of crashes involving teenagers driving drunk after school proms and graduation parties.[6]

This has led many communities to hold "safe and sober" graduation parties designed to keep teenagers away from alcohol and off the road. These chaperoned all-night parties are alcohol free, and attendees are required to stay on the premises for the duration of the party.[7]

Feeling Invincible

Leah Bean used to drink. She enjoyed partying with her friends. She says that she and her friends felt invincible, "as if there's a bubble around fifteen-to-twenty-one-year-olds that prevents bad things from happening."[8] But during her junior year in high school, the bubble burst.

A group of her friends got liquor at a store notorious for not checking IDs. Leah's best friend, April, got drunk. She got into a car with a nineteen-year-old driver who was also drunk. Later tests showed that the driver had a blood alcohol content of .20, more than twice the adult legal limit in their home state of Tennessee. The driver crashed the car. April died. Now Leah does not drink anymore. But she does not have her best friend, either.[9]

Kevin Morey began drinking as a teenager. He was used to driving while under the influence. He says, "People used to tell me I was good at driving drunk, so I never really worried about what could happen."[10]

One night when he was twenty years old, he went to a party with his best friend, David. The party got loud, and police arrived to tell them to keep the noise down, but no one was arrested for being drunk.

Later, Kevin decided to drive three of his friends home. He was drunk and lost control of the vehicle. The car flipped over. Two of the kids jumped out in time, but David had passed out from drinking. He fell on the pavement with the car on top of him. Kevin recalls, "I remember struggling to get out of the car. Then my friend screamed, 'Oh my God, David's under the car!' I saw him lying there, pinned under the car. He was vomiting, so I figured that meant he was alive."

But he was not. David was dead.

Kevin pleaded guilty in court and was convicted of negligent homicide. He was sentenced to a year in jail and six months of community service. While he was in jail, he completed an Alcoholics

Deadly car accidents can be one tragic result of alcohol misuse.

Anonymous program. He now speaks in schools trying to prevent other teens from making the same mistakes he did.

Kevin says, "I definitely deserved punishment. The crash isn't something I should have gotten away with. What I did was serious. I've lost years of my life, but that doesn't equal the loss that David's family will have forever."[11]

Brooke Blanchard was an active seventeen-year-old who was a class officer and a star soccer player. She was killed by a sixteen-year-old drunk driver. Because the driver was under age, the killer received no jail time.

Brooke's mother, Ginger Blanchard, worked for three years to get the laws in her state of New Hampshire changed. She also began speaking at schools, showing other teens the prom dress that Brooke never got to wear. She says remembering her daughter trying on the dress hurts, but she says, "If the sight of that dress makes one girl or young man realize it could happen to them if they drink and drive, it's worth the pain."

The Brooke Blanchard law was passed in January 1999. It says that anyone under the age of seventeen who is convicted of a negligent motor vehicle homicide can be tried as an adult. Brooke's family is happy the law is in effect, but Ginger Blanchard says, "I'd much rather have a daughter than a law."[12]

Liquor Industry Criticized

The liquor industry has received strong criticism for its role in the alcohol problem. Their advertising techniques have come under fire. In 1999, the Federal Trade Commission (FTC) reported to Congress on this issue in response to public concern over advertising's role in underage drinking. The FTC recommended that the liquor industry, which regulates itself on advertising, adopt stricter guidelines.[13]

A September 2002 report by the Center on Alcohol Marketing and Youth at Georgetown University claims that youths ages twelve to twenty see 45 percent more beer advertisements in magazines and 27 percent more liquor advertisements than do adults.[14]

Jim O'Hara, the center's executive director, said, "America's parents should be disturbed by these findings. They aren't seeing these ads but their children are because that's where the industry is putting them—in the magazines their children read."[15]

Some of the magazines mentioned, such as *Rolling Stone, Sports Illustrated,* and *In Style,* have an adult market, but teens also read them. Liquor industry officials reject the findings, claiming the group's definition of a youth-oriented magazine is much too strict. Dan Tearno, then vice president for corporate affairs at Heineken USA, said his company advertises only in magazines whose audiences are, for the most part, old enough to drink.

But the study group considered those magazines to be aimed at readers younger than twenty-one. As Jim O'Hara said:

"We have shown that the industry is falling far short of the kind of steps that the FTC said should be taken to protect youth. If you want to reduce your underage exposure, you would probably choose not to advertise in certain magazines, this is a choice you make because you want to be responsible. . . . I think the actions of these companies speak very loudly."[16]

In response to the 2002 study, the Beer Institute issued a statement saying it does not target underage consumers. It said, "The way to address illegal underage drinking is to encourage others to get behind programs that are working instead of wasting valuable time censoring advertising to adults of legal drinking age."[17]

Sweet Taste, Bad Backlash

Another study, by the National Center on Addiction and Substance Abuse (CASA), criticizes alcohol marketers for the new wave of sweet-tasting malt alternative beverages known as alcopops, saying they are a creeping scourge among teenagers. They say these drinks, such as hard lemonades and flavored wine coolers, are marketed with advertising images that appeal to children. The study also claims drinkers under the age of twenty-one account for 25 percent of all alcohol consumed in the United States.[18]

Some refute these statistics as exaggerated and say that the report is "flat out wrong."[19] A spokesman for the Distilled Spirits Council of the United States says, "We decry any under twenty-one alcohol consumption," and goes on to claim that underage drinking is on the decline. He also points out that the spirits industry has spent more than $120 million during the past ten years to help combat the problem.[20]

The CASA report included some strong recommendations, such as a ban on television alcohol advertising, higher alcohol taxes, and the inclusion of alcohol in the White House Office of National Drug Control Policy's media campaigns.[21]

Issues of Trust

One important factor in the teen drinking issue is parental responsibility. Parents need to be aware of the extent of their kids' activities. Many people feel that they should be held responsible for the consequences of their teenagers' actions.

One father of a teenage daughter has a unique perspective. As a teacher, his students tell him what really goes on at teen parties. One confessed to him that many kids drink to get drunk as fast as they can and the designated driver is often the one who "only has four beers."[22]

Some parents assume they are keeping tabs on their kids by being in touch by cell phone. In reality, the cell phones can enable the kids to deceive their parents about their true whereabouts and the location of unchaperoned parties. "Cell phones and [other devices] are major arteries of communications—of spreading the word where the best parties are," explains one girl.[23]

Mixed Feelings

Some parents are aware of their teens' drinking habits but are afraid of making an issue of it. A single father feels his practical approach works best. He knows his eighteen-year-old daughter drinks beer at her friends' homes, but he will not allow drinking in his own house. He says, "If kids are going to experiment, isn't it better that they do it when they're still living at home, where there is some parental influence?"[24]

A like-minded mother echoes the sentiment. With conflicting emotions, she threw her son an eighteenth birthday party. She decided not to provide alcohol but knew some of his friends would bring it to the house. Her husband stood watch as the party ended and made sure no one who had been drinking was driving. She explained her reasoning:

"If you have a kid who chooses to be social, you make a choice between absolutely forbidding drinking and having him lie to you, or allowing him to do a certain amount of drinking and knowing about it. I have very mixed feelings about it and I know I'm not alone."[25]

The problem of underage drinking is difficult for parents and communities to solve because alcohol is widely available at parties.

Jeff Levy could not disagree more. His son Travis began drinking on occasion around the age of fifteen. His father would punish him; he would quit for a while, then go back to his old habits. When Travis entered college, he continued to drink. He was cited for underage drinking but did not, or could not, stop. He swore he would cut down on his drinking and would not do anything stupid. One night he had been drinking and got into a car driven by a friend who was also under the influence. Their car slammed into another car, killing them both and the other driver.

Travis's father is sorry he did not take stronger steps against his son's drinking when it began. "Parents need to make it very clear, there will be zero tolerance on this issue," he says. "Right now, kids understand that everyone is soft on alcohol."[26] Levy now travels the country spreading his story and message.

One mother did take strong steps when she caught her fifteen-year-old daughter on three separate occasions coming home after a party smelling of beer. At first, she tried contacting the parties' hosts, and then she tried grounding her daughter. After the third time, she bought a Breathalyzer over the Internet. She told her daughter that if she suspected any more drinking, she would use it. Her intervention worked. The mother had no further problems from the girl.[27] Is this a harsh action or proper parenting?

New Laws, New Attitudes

Current legislation may make stricter parenting necessary. In some states, laws are being passed that punish the parents or other adult providers and make them liable if their children drink. In Minnesota, those convicted under the ZAP law (Zero Adult Providers) can be jailed, fined, or sued for damages. In North Carolina, anyone convicted of providing alcohol to underage persons will be fined a minimum of two hundred fifty dollars and assigned twenty-five hours of community service. In Maryland, adult providers can be charged up to one thousand dollars for a first offense.

Increased awareness and responsibility is the goal. The thinking is that if parents know they are also at risk of punishment, they will restrict their own actions and the actions of their teens. They cannot claim ignorance of what is going on in their own homes or condone alcohol use.[28]

A social host law in Boston holds any host responsible for the actions of a guest who becomes drunk. Eric Norlin, age seventeen, and Dennis Richardson, age twenty, faced criminal charges stemming from a 2003 incident where they held a party in Norlin's home while his parents were away. Three girls brought liquor to the party and became drunk. Upon leaving around 2:00 A.M., Shannon Dwyer, age nineteen, died after her car struck a tree.

Norlin's lawyer argued that Eric should not be held responsible. He said, "What gives this kid control over the residence? He has no control because his parents weren't home."[29]

Don Smith spearheaded the legislation after his own son died in a drunk-driving accident. He had been at a party where adults allegedly played drinking games with minors. Smith feels that Norlin and Richardson should be punished. He says, "Maybe parents will be more aware of what their kids are doing while they are away, and maybe kids will think twice before serving alcohol or allowing kids to drink in their house."[30]

In some communities, parents can also be held liable regardless of whether they knew of the party or not. Parents can also be held responsible even if they were not on the premises themselves.[31]

When Gary Finger was the mayor of the township of Voorhees, New Jersey, he persuaded the township officials to purchase one thousand saliva swab kits that test for blood-alcohol content and offered it to parents for free. He hoped that if parents had the option to test their kids for drinking, they would be able to identify or avoid a problem. The kits generated controversy. The kids felt it was simply an example of stronger control, a violation of their privacy, and a lack of trust.

Police lieutenant Jeff Nardello of the township suggested that parents "should discuss this test with their children long before they use it. I wouldn't use it as a surprise. I would use it as a deterrent."[32]

Frank Winters, a member of the board of national directors of MADD, agrees and is glad the tests are available. He says, "People have to understand that alcohol is the number-one choice of drugs in this country, and it's readily available."[33]

Drinking is like any other addiction—it is difficult to tell how quickly or likely someone is to get hooked. Statistics show teens who drink put themselves at risk—of addiction, of long-term health problems, and of the devastating effects of car accidents. Long-term health risks are involved. Drinking and driving destroys many young lives, tragically proving how dangerous alcohol is. Teens need to be aware that their actions have consequences and that they are responsible for them.

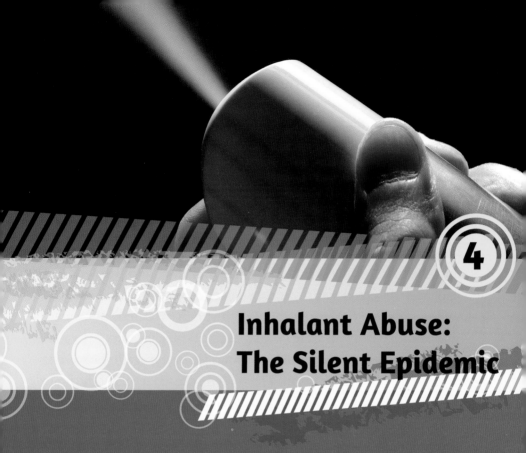

Inhalant Abuse: The Silent Epidemic

Inhalant abuse, or "huffing," has been called the silent epidemic. It differs from other substance abuse in very significant ways. The products used to obtain a high are cheap, readily available, found in every home, and legal for minors to obtain. Huffing is also the most common form of abuse among children age eight to twelve. Research indicates that inhalant abusers are more likely to abuse other substances later in life.[1]

The practice of sniffing, or huffing, substances has been recognized for decades. The products used by huffers are usually common household solvents such as gasoline, lighter fluid, glue, correction fluid, paint thinner, air freshener, and fingernail polish. This makes abuse easy. There is no need to find a drug dealer, make an illegal purchase, or risk being caught by police. Inhalant abuse cannot be detected through blood or urine tests, which makes it easier to keep secret.[2]

Kids try inhalants for many reasons. Curiosity and peer pressure can be factors. Huffers often do not believe anything bad can happen. They think it is a harmless way to get high, and they begin to crave the experience. They easily get hooked.

Huffers report having a euphoric feeling, a sense of escape from boredom or any problems they may have. This is because inhalants act quickly on the brain, causing changes.

For example, scientists using advanced technology and an imaging process studied how toluene, a common solvent, seeped into the brain. They scanned the brains of mice and baboons that had been injected with the substance. The images showed that toluene affected the same regions in the brain as cocaine does, areas that are linked to pleasure. When euphoric feelings are activated, people want to experience those feelings again and again. This is one reason why addictions begin. The toluene caused levels of the brain chemical dopamine (which is associated with euphoric feelings) to fluctuate. The toluene then moved through the rest of the brain before being cleared out of the body by the kidneys. The scientists also collected tissue samples to reinforce the image findings.[3]

Dr. Janet F. Williams, a member of the American Academy of Pediatrics committee on substance abuse, tells how dangerous the changes are. "There are several classes of inhalants and they basically act as solvents and cause permanent neurological damage. It's irreversible."[4]

The brain damage, memory loss, and other problems caused by huffing can hurt academic performance. A federal survey showed that kids age twelve to seventeen who reported a D average in school were three times more likely to have huffed during the previous year than kids with an A average.[5]

Methods Used

The methods of using inhalants are simple and dangerous. Many abusers simply sniff or breathe fumes from open containers to get high. Sometimes liquid solvents are put into plastic bottles or aluminum cans and then inhaled. To increase the concentration of vapors and get a stronger effect, some liquid solvents are poured onto a rag or into a bag and held over the nose and mouth and breathed in.

Tyler James Pinnick, a twelve-year-old boy, died after inhaling air freshener fumes from an aerosol can. Tyler had often discussed alcohol and illegal drugs with his mother. "We talked openly," she said. "But I'd never heard of 'huffing.'"[6]

While visiting his great-grandmother's home, Tyler locked himself in the bathroom and, after sniffing the air freshener, passed out. His great-grandmother called paramedics, but they were unable to revive the boy.

Tyler's death devastated his family. They could not understand why he had been huffing. His father grieves but passes no judgment. "He wasn't a depressed kid, or in any trouble," he says. "It could have been boredom; it could have been peer pressure. I just can't judge those kids. The thing is, he was alone."[7]

Hidden Dangers

What caused Tyler to die? Medical experts say sniffing or huffing can prevent oxygen from entering the bloodstream. This can occur immediately and result in damaged organs, blackouts, or death.[8]

Even for first-time users, inhalants can be addictive—or fatal. They can trigger a dangerously irregular heartbeat. Earl Siegel, co-director of the drug and poison information center at the Cincinnati Children's Hospital Medical Center, describes what happens to some huffers. "They seem in good shape—they may be laughing or giddy, and then several minutes later they're dead."[9]

Dr. H. Westley Clark, director of the Center for Substance Abuse Treatment, warns that many parents are reluctant to speak to their children about inhalant abuse and may even be in denial. He says, "A lot of children are experimenting, so if you assume it's not your kid you'd better check."[10]

A recent survey found that nearly 2 million young kids and teens in the United States reported using inhalants to get high at least once in their life. That is nearly 9 percent of all American youth. Statistics also show a rise in first-time users, indicating that a dangerous trend may be emerging.[11] Huffing now ranks fourth in all substance abuse cases among young people between ages twelve to seventeen, directly behind alcohol, tobacco, and marijuana.[12]

Clark also has suggestions for detecting possible abuse: "Watch for changes in behavior—personality changes, changes in gait, chemical breath, secretive and isolated behavior—that may signal inhalant use."[13] Other signs include paint stains on clothing, red or runny eyes, a drunken or dizzy appearance, and sores around the mouth.

How Many Die?

It is impossible to know how many teens die because of huffing. Many deaths simply get written off as suicides or accidents. The National Inhalant Prevention Coalition gets reports of about 100 to 125 deaths per year caused by huffing. But Dr. Harvey Weiss, the executive director of the organization, believes that those numbers vastly underestimate the problem.[14]

Unfortunately, inhalant abuse sometimes is not widely discussed publicly until tragedy strikes. A fatal car crash in Philadelphia proved to be a wake-up call for one community and thrust the problem of huffing into national attention. Five high school girls lost their lives. The coroner's reports showed that inhalant abuse was a factor: Four of the five girls, including the driver of the car, had ingested significant amounts of a computer keyboard cleaner.

After the accident, the phone mailbox at the National Inhalant Prevention Coalition received more than one thousand calls. And the group's Web site received more than three times that number of hits from the media and from parents seeking more information about inhalant abuse.[15]

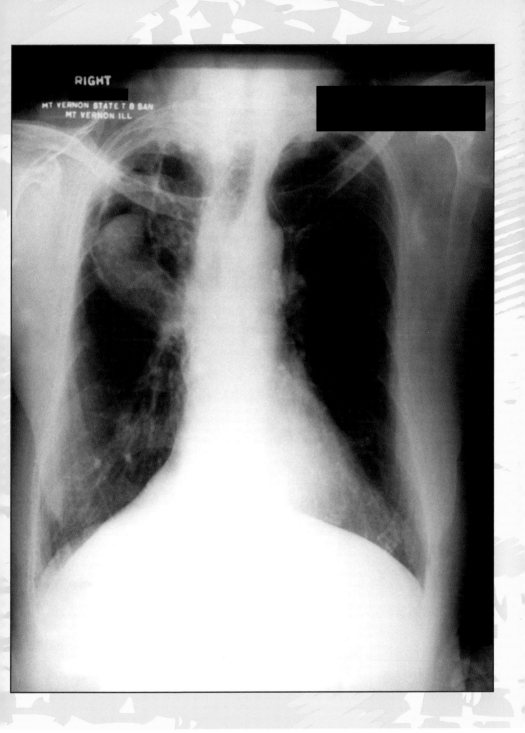

Inhalant abuse can damage the brain, heart, kidneys, and lungs. This lung X ray shows damage to the upper right lung, which can lead to respiratory illness and death.

Elaine Franklin's lack of knowledge about inhalant abuse proved tragic. Her thirteen-year-old son, Anthony, died after huffing air freshener. Elaine admits she knew he had experimented. "I knew he had done this once before, but he said he would never try it again. He promised me; he swore up and down. If I had ever even heard of sniffing death, I would have been extremely concerned, but I didn't know."[16]

A Cycle of Abuse

Andrew Robert Sandy confessed to his mother that he had been huffing Freon, a common gas found in home heating and cooling systems, since he was seven years old and an older friend showed him how to do it. When he was ten years old, he also began smoking marijuana. At the age of twelve, he was arrested for possession.

At that point, Andrew decided to go back to using inhalants to get high because they do not show up on drug screening tests. When he was under the influence, he lost control. His mother was often a witness to this. She said, "He could be so sweet, but when he was high, he was violent."[17]

Andrew kicked holes in the patio at his home and banged his head against a door so hard he left a dent in it. One day, he threatened a teacher at his middle school and was locked up in a youth facility. Upon his release, he went right back to abusing inhalants.

One night, Andrew was found unconscious in his room. He had a plastic garbage bag over his head. He was rushed to the local hospital, where he died. Traces of Freon were found in his body, and authorities attributed his death to huffing. They determined that Andrew had filled the bag with Freon and inhaled it in his room.

"The abuse destroyed my son's life," his mother said.[18] He was thirteen years old and had been huffing for six years.

Few Options Available

Unfortunately, huffers have few options available to them to get help after an episode. "One of the big problems is that there are very,

very few treatment centers," Weiss explains. "I've tried really hard to find someplace for them, but very few places are set up to deal with huffers."[19]

Abusers do not often go to local drug treatment centers for help. If they do end up in a facility, their problem is not acknowledged as huffing. Mitzi Ross, of the Montgomery Department of Health and Human Services in Maryland (Andrew's home state), explains, "[Huffing is] almost never listed as the reason for their being brought in. They aren't discovered. They aren't cited or arrested for it."[20]

Is huffing being overlooked or even ignored? Are counselors experienced enough to recognize and differentiate huffing from other forms of addictions? These questions are being asked by many agencies and others concerned with youth and substance abuse in all forms.

What should you do if you find someone in a crisis? Try to remain calm and call for emergency help before you do anything else. Huffers under the influence may become violent or experience hallucinations. Make sure the room is well ventilated. If the person is not breathing, administer CPR. Get professional medical help immediately, and after recovery, encourage the person to get help for the problem.[21]

Education Is Effective

When the risks of huffing are discussed openly, usage drops. Harvey Weiss shares his experience, saying, "Children are fifty percent less likely to huff if their parents talk to them about the dangers of inhalants."[22]

He also points out the many instances where government-sponsored education programs have had significant impact. Unfortunately, the programs often stop due to loss of funding.

Texas, for example, saw a 50 percent reduction in inhalant use among elementary school students during the four years a state commission funded an aggressive inhalant abuse prevention program. When funds were cut and the program ended, usage increased by 50 percent during the next four years. Essentially, all progress gained was lost.

Nationally, with the support of many antidrug groups, one week in March has been declared National Inhalants and Poison Awareness Week. The hope is this will help draw attention to the problem of huffing and the many dangers household chemicals pose.[23]

Most surveys, reports, and studies point to the same conclusion: The key to keeping kids from ever beginning the dangerous practice of huffing is to educate them and to begin at a young age. Elementary age children should be taught that the substances used are poisonous and can be fatal.

Dr. Janet F. Williams feels the brain images that show damage due to inhalants could have an impact on children. She thinks that pictures have more impact on students than do facts and figures or general warnings of danger. She also supports the idea that educating children about the dangers of huffing at an early age is crucial. She says, "By middle to late teens, they've usually stopped, died, or gone on to something else."[24]

Smoking: Not Just a Bad Habit

Three thousand American teens start smoking each day. Many will become lifetime smokers. It is the nicotine found in cigarettes that is so addictive. This drug stimulates nerve cells, making the smoker feel either anxious or relaxed. Once tolerance is built up, dependence sets in. Smokers increase the number of cigarettes they smoke per day, and they can become hooked on the habit.

Sean, a seventeen-year-old, first tried smoking at the age of twelve. The experience was not pleasant. "I liked fitting in with the older kids," he admits. "But I didn't feel so good."[1] However, Sean was soon using cigarettes to relax and escape from his everyday life.

The group of kids he associated with did not just use cigarettes. Sean began experimenting with drugs and alcohol. He ended up in a drug and alcohol rehabilitation program. Getting clean was tough, but he made it—except for cigarettes. It was the one addiction he could not conquer.

Sean entered a seven-week program called SOS (Stop Our Smoking) specifically designed to help people stop smoking. Kathy White, designer and facilitator of the program, explains how it motivates teens to quit:

"We talk about the physical addiction that comes with smoking—the craving—the way the body itches to satisfy itself with a cigarette—and the psychological addiction. How it comforts, distracts, decreases stress—and how cigarettes become a best friend."[2]

She explains some of the methods the program uses to help habitual smokers quit:

"The teens work diligently on problem solving and choose alternative behaviors to stop incidences of smoking. Talking helps, so does deep breathing, carrying a straw to chew on, or wearing a rubber band around your wrist and snapping it when you feel an urge to smoke."[3]

For Sean, the SOS message finally got through. "In SOS, something just clicked," he said. "I started caring about my body, my diet—and I started weight training. SOS taught me the benefits of quitting, had me list the pros and cons. The pros outweighed the cons, so I threw my cigarettes out the window and quit."[4]

He also regrets how much money he wasted buying cigarettes. "Outside of the health risks, it's ridiculous—the amount of money I blew smoking. I've done the math. I could have taken a helicopter to school every day with the money I spent on cigarettes."[5]

Hooked

Just as with other addictions, teens get hooked on cigarettes much more quickly than adult smokers. A recent study sponsored by the National Cancer Institute revealed some startling results about young smokers. The in-depth research was based on student interviews. The kids, ages twelve and thirteen, were checked three times per year for thirty months regarding the duration of their smoking, the frequency, quantity, and similar factors. The researchers also looked for other signs of dependence, including smoking in places they were not supposed to (such as school), finding it hard to concentrate without smoking, and irritability when denied cigarettes.

Dr. Joseph R. DiFranza of the University of Massachusetts led the study. He reports:

> Everything we knew (about smoking in teens) was wrong. I thought that kids who got hooked quickly would be the exception to the rule. As it turned out, the kids who did not get hooked quickly were the exception. . . . Some of these kids were hooked within a few days of starting to smoke.[6]

The time for symptoms of addiction to set in was 21 days for girls and 183 days for boys. What is even more surprising is that the symptoms began when the frequency of smoking was only two cigarettes one day per week. The data showed that even at these low levels, the kids who showed signs of being hooked were forty-four times more likely to still be smoking at the end of the study. DiFranza speculates that the still-developing adolescent brain makes teens more vulnerable to the effects of nicotine, and therefore to addiction, than adults.[7]

The Power of Nicotine

Why are cigarettes so addictive? The effects of nicotine are subtle. The smoker may feel relaxed and derive pleasure from smoking, but smokers do not report a "high" or feelings of euphoria that addicts describe when using harder drugs. Yet abstaining from cigarettes is much more difficult for some people than kicking a drug habit.

One theory of why this occurs is based on the number of times smokers "dose" themselves with their drug of choice. For example, a pack-a-day smoker would receive approximately two hundred doses every day. (This is based on an average of ten puffs per cigarette multiplied by twenty cigarettes per day.) Smokers dose themselves

Recent research has shown that young people get hooked on cigarettes much faster than adults do, and girls become addicted more quickly than boys.

with nicotine hundreds of thousands of times over their smoking careers—a number unrivaled in any other drug habit.[8]

The health risks involved with this number of dosages are serious. Smoking is harmful in many ways. Most people are aware that smoking can cause lung cancer, but it also makes the bronchial tubes smaller, which can result in chronic bronchitis.

Smoking restricts blood vessels, which contributes to high blood pressure and heart disease. The entire body gets less oxygen, and the blood flow to the brain is decreased, which can cause mood swings. Smoking can also cause stomach ulcers and digestive problems.

Along with the increased chance of oral cancer, smoking also causes bad breath, discolored teeth and skin, and wrinkles.[9]

Women who smoke and become pregnant also face the added risks of having babies with low birth weight and developmental problems. Additionally, research shows that girls become addicted more easily than boys.[10] They are also more likely to die of lung cancer than males who smoke the same number of cigarettes.[11] In fact, a recent report from the surgeon general states there has been a 600 percent increase in women's death rates from lung cancer since 1950, and that those deaths are a direct result of a smoking addiction that begins in childhood. It is estimated that smoking among women causes more than 165,000 preventable deaths each year.[12]

Reversing the Risk

The benefits of stopping smoking are considerable, and many are immediate. The carbon monoxide found in cigarettes inhibits the red blood cells from carrying oxygen efficiently to the body. Within one day of quitting, carbon monoxide blood levels fall, and the body gets the oxygen it needs.

Statistics can vary depending on the age when a person began smoking and other factors, but they still show that there are remarkable reversals of health risks for those able to kick the habit. Smokers have a 70 percent increased risk of heart attack over nonsmokers, but within one year of quitting, the risk is cut in half. After fifteen smoke-free years, the risk of heart attack is as low as it is for a person who has never smoked.

Smokers also have a seven to twenty times greater chance of developing lung cancer than nonsmokers. After ten years of abstinence, the risk drops by half. After fifteen years, the former smoker has a risk for lung cancer of about four times that of a nonsmoker.[13]

Even knowing the risks and being aware of the benefits of quitting does not stop smokers from lighting up. Why?

A teenager from Virginia told a panel of experts on smoking why she believed teens smoked: "Kids are going to smoke no matter what the laws are because they rebel and because it's cool. I think kids need parents to instill in them that they can be comfortable with themselves. I think that's why kids start smoking."[14]

Can a parent's influence override the strong messages advertisers send that present smoking as a desirable escape, a companionable pastime, and a mark of sophistication? The question of parental involvement and criticism of advertisers are pivotal points in the smoking controversy.

Advertising Targets

Antismoking advocates believe that cigarette manufacturers (banned by law since 1988 from using billboards to sell their products) have shifted their focus to small local convenience markets and gas stations. These are places often frequented by teenagers and children. Referred to as point-of-purchase advertising, their methods place ads in key locations such as candy aisles and near cash registers.

An antitobacco education group sent fifty-four teenagers into two hundred fifty markets, convenience stores, and gas stations throughout three California counties to test their theory. The teens counted the number of cigarette ads found. Although their findings fluctuated depending on the communities canvassed, the numbers were significant. On average, they saw up to twenty advertisements per location.[15]

Kate Barton, age fifteen, helped gather the information. She expressed her surprise: "It was shocking to me that I didn't ever notice it before. It made you feel almost angry that they were so shamelessly trying to target little kids."[16]

Jan Smith, a spokeswoman for R.J. Reynolds Tobacco Company, the country's second-largest cigarette manufacturer, denies that this type of advertising has a strong impact on underage smokers. "We do not want youth to smoke—period," she says. "If you look at all the studies, the primary influence on children who make the mistake of smoking is peer or family influence. It's not the advertising."[17]

But Fernando Gonzalez, age sixteen, had his eyes opened after being a part of the experiment. He said, "Kids were going into these stores, passing by all the ads, and on the other side was the candy. I wouldn't want my kids even going to these stores."[18]

A New Message

In response to such criticism, tobacco companies began their own antismoking campaigns. Michael E. Szymanczyk of the Philip Morris Company says their efforts to combat underage smoking are entirely sincere. "If you're a decent person, you don't want kids to

New antismoking programs are aimed at ensuring that young people never start smoking.

smoke. You don't want them to do something that's going to harm them." He goes on to say the antismoking campaign is not only for the community but is in the cigarette company's best interest. "In order for this business to exist successfully in this society, we had to accept at least some responsibility for deterring kids from smoking."[19]

The advertising spots designed for television have two main themes: that you do not have to smoke to be cool and that most kids do not smoke. They are tested extensively in focus groups and by surveys including both parents and children. The company evaluates the feedback gathered.

Some of the feedback was not favorable. One commercial never aired because response from kids pointed out the girl who was being interviewed about why she did not smoke looked like she was lying. They also said her makeup "made her look like a smoker."[20]

The company decided to change their approach. Instead of using teenagers to spread their message to other teens, their new ads will target parents directly, urging them to get involved in their kids' lives and talk to them about not smoking.[21]

Attacking Teens' Wallets

The Centers for Disease Control and Prevention reports that smoking among U.S. high school students has dropped to the lowest level in a decade. But the rate is still hovering at around 29 percent.[22]

In California, legislation proposing higher taxes on cigarettes may help combat the problem. Studies have shown that teens are especially sensitive to price increases. The last time that state increased taxes by fifty cents per pack, the smoking rate among teens ages twelve to seventeen fell by 35.5 percent. This proves that tax hikes can have a direct impact, and that may be essential in keeping young smokers from becoming lifelong smokers.[23]

According to the CDC, every pack of cigarettes sold in the United States costs more than seven dollars in medical care and lost productivity. This amounts to more than $157 billion per year.[24]

There are other deterrents that have also proven effective. Research from the National Cancer Institute shows tightening laws that restrict access to tobacco—and enforcing these laws— is another method that works. Their study also showed that antismoking campaigns did have a slight effect, backing up the claims of the cigarette manufacturers.[25]

Kicking the Habit

Nicotine replacement therapies such as gum, inhalers, spray, and patches can help smokers quit. They help reduce cravings often experienced during withdrawal. The therapies work by releasing monitored doses of nicotine, then gradually reducing the dosage until the smoker is nicotine free. By eliminating the need for nicotine, hopefully, the smoker can eliminate cigarettes.

Other self-help methods include:

- Committing to quit verbally so friends and family are aware of the decision.

- Making a list of the reasons for becoming smoke free.

- Picking a date to stop smoking—and sticking to it.

- Keeping a journal to identify the times one feels an urge to smoke, such as after a meal or during stress. (Identifying triggers helps a person through the difficult periods.)

- Changing habits and choosing other options, such as chewing gum after a meal rather than smoking.

- Seeking support for the decision to quit—talking with others—can help.[26]

Some of the biggest success stories show the importance of motivation. One fifteen-year-old who had been smoking since the age of ten found the strength to quit only after realizing how his addiction influenced his little brother:

I had just started the tenth grade when I saw my little brother smoking. I told him to put the cigarette out, that it was wrong for him to be smoking. He said, "You do it! Why can't I?" My little brother had a point. And I didn't have an answer. If I smoke, why can't he? I decided that I had to quit smoking. I told my little brother that having fun is better than smoking. I did a lot of things with him. I showed him more creative things to do than smoke. We began to exercise together, play baseball, run track. When we stopped smoking, we got closer. After I quit, I began to feel better. I had more energy. My stamina improved. I didn't tire as easily. I felt more motivated.[27]

The teen also began working with a group that brings the antismoking message into junior high schools. And he is trying to help his mother stop her smoking habit.

Realizing the harm teens cause to themselves and others is the first and possibly most important step to stopping the smoking habit before it becomes a serious addiction.

Eating Disorders: Deadly Behavior

Eating disorders are growing among teenagers. Anorexia and bulimia offer a false sense of control and a way to gain acceptance in a society obsessed with being thin. They are addictive behaviors that take over and ruin lives. Anorexics and bulimics go to great lengths to practice their addictions while keeping them a secret.

Bulimics will consume vast quantities of food, usually by themselves out of sight of others. They binge uncontrollably, then purge (getting rid of the food by vomiting, using laxatives and diuretics, or overexercising). As in any other addiction, the pattern is repeated over and over.

Anorexics take dieting to the extreme, sometimes restricting calories to the point of starvation. Sometimes excessive exercise and strict workout schedules rule their day-to-day existence.[1]

Some people practice both bulimia and anorexia in a drastic attempt to control their weight. They usually deny they have a problem. They feel that their obsession with food is acceptable. They are only trying to conform to society's ideal body image.

Jen's Story

For two years, beginning at age thirteen, anorexia took over Jen Shallo's life. She began her eighth-grade school year at a healthy one hundred fifteen pounds on her 5'3" frame. In six months, she dropped twenty-five pounds. She continued to lose weight; at her lowest point she weighed only sixty-five pounds.

As a recovering anorexic, Jen talks to teens at her old high school, hoping to spread information and warn others. Jen's problem began during her middle school years, and she knows that educating kids at younger ages is also important. She does not mind using herself as an example. She says, "Kids need to know, fourth graders need to know. It's better to stand up there and show and tell than do nothing. Nobody is ever bored by my story."[2]

Louise Miller, a middle school psychologist, agrees, noting that kids are often more aware than adults of another teen's eating disorder. "Once it becomes painfully obvious, friends come forward, but not parents. Either they [the parents] are not aware or they're in denial."[3]

Miller believes that discussing the issue with a recovering anorexic like Jen might help save many young teens from the horrors of an eating disorder.

Image Is Everything

Women and young girls are bombarded daily with images of extremely thin models selling everything from perfume to cigarettes, shoes, and cars. This "thin is in" brand of advertising began in the mid-1960s when a seventeen-year-old model from England entered the American fashion scene. The 5-foot 6-inch girl weighed only ninety-seven pounds and was nicknamed "Twiggy." She became an instant celebrity, and women tried to be like her, dieting to become extremely thin. Experts point to this era as the beginning of eating disorders.[4]

Another major influence over young girls is the Barbie doll. Popular since the late 1950s, Barbie has body dimensions not found in real women. Her breasts are overly large, her hips slim, her waist tiny, and her legs impossibly long and slender.

A researcher spoke to a group of nine-year-old girls who owned Barbies about how older girls might feel concerning their bodies. The young girls were able to associate the perfect image of the doll with the possible negative feelings girls might develop if they did not fit that image. One girl named Monica wrote to the Mattel toy company about her feelings:

> *Dear Mattel:*
>
> *Make your Barbie dolls less adorable or stop selling them because little kids and older kids and even younger sisters and brothers play with Barbie dolls and in one second they will want to look as skinny as them. So either stop selling them or make them more normal, a little chubbier, not as big boobed and not standing on their tippy toes. Make more pants, and not only shirts with puffy shoulders which come down to their belly buttons. Make full bathing suits and not only bikini bathing suits.*[5]

Another critical factor in a young girl's body image comes during the onset of puberty. At this time, girls experience a 20 to 30 percent increase in body fat. Many are anxious about the changes their bodies are going through. They are embarrassed and confused. Conflicting emotions about growing up and their new appearance are brought to the forefront during puberty. Some girls turn to eating disorders in an attempt to stop the unwelcome process.[6]

Obese Teens

Another disorder faced by many teens today is obesity—defined as having a body weight more than 20 to 25 percent higher than the maximum ideal weight for their height. Morbid obesity is a term that refers to those who are more than 100 pounds overweight. The American Academy of Child and Adolescent Psychiatry reports that 16 to 33 percent of American teenagers are obese. They are at risk of developing type 2 diabetes, protein deficiency, heart disease, and cancer.[7]

Junk foods and a marked decrease in physical activity are part of the cause, but other factors must be considered as well. There is a direct link between overeating, stress, and painful emotions. Some teens overeat instead of dealing with the issues that bother them. Most professionals believe that until the underlying problems are dealt with, an obese teen will never successfully lose weight. Support groups such as Overeaters Anonymous can help.[8]

More research is needed to help the medical profession decide what the best treatments are for morbidly obese teens. And teenagers facing the problem need to help discover why they overeat and how they can stop. It is a serious condition with serious consequences.

Trying to Cope

Some teens with eating disorders use them as a mechanism to cope with severe stress. Many have a history of trauma such as sexual or physical abuse. Controlling their food gives them a feeling of empowerment. It serves as a substitute for the lack of control in other areas of their lives. Rejecting food, for example, may send a message to their family and gain attention. Overeating may soothe their emotional pain. Purging food may be a means to vent anger and frustration.[9]

The link between eating disorders and emotional problems is crucial. Emotional distress is the reason those with disorders abuse their bodies. Weight loss is not the true motivation. The underlying issues must be addressed in order to deal with the disorder and break the cycle.

Kim, an anorexic, explains how her overwhelming family problems led to her addictive behavior and her decision to eat no more than three hundred calories per day:

My parents had gotten separated freshmen year, my dad remarried that summer and my mom had gotten cancer. There was a tremendous amount of anger, pain that I didn't deal with. I have two brothers and a sister, and everyone took a different route to deal with all of these things that were happening— trauma, basically. And I was always an internal person. My sister is quicker and lets out anger, and I didn't do that as much. So I just sort of went into my own little world, I think. And then that world became totally about eating and weight.[10]

Starving for Attention

In the early 1970s, long before much was known about eating disorders, Cherry Boone, the daughter of a celebrity, began her own battle against anorexia and bulimia. Cherry's father, Pat Boone, was a well-known singer, and Cherry and her family often performed with him.

She had every material thing she wanted and was an overachiever in school. But her anxieties about living up to her parents' expectations and her own lack of self-esteem led her to binge and purge. She also went for long periods on near-starvation diets and a grueling exercise program to control her weight. On a typical day, Cherry barely ate enough food to make up one good meal and maintained an exercise schedule that was astounding. She would jog four miles in the morning and do stretching exercises. In the afternoon, she would walk her dog for an hour and spend two hours doing calisthenics and weight lifting. She would also swim laps and do leg exercises for forty-five minutes.[11]

Cherry was eventually hospitalized at eighty pounds and struggled for years and through several relapses before overcoming her problems. After her long recovery, she wrote the book *Starving for Attention*, which chronicled her experiences.

People in today's society—especially young women—are under constant pressure to conform to an unrealistically thin image.

Immigrant Girls in Conflict

Recent studies indicate another alarming trend involving immigrant girls who develop eating disorders trying to fit in and look "American."

Dee Park, of Asian decent, was teased at school about her muscular body. Kids laughed at her and told her Asians were supposed to "look smaller." Dee turned to bulimia and anorexia. She remembers her struggle and realizes her problems were compounded by her race. She said:

> Being Korean, I felt that I looked very different from everyone and that I wanted to fit in and be perfect and have that good, really skinny body. I look back on my life and I see all these different factors that led to my bulimia and anorexia. Being an immigrant in this country was a major one.[12]

Lori Charnee's family came from the Ukraine. Since the age of fifteen she has suffered from anorexia. She is now thirty years old. Lori's feelings echo those of many immigrant girls: "The biggest pressure I felt was that the family sacrificed everything to come here. You feel like you need to make something of yourself. You are expected to succeed and pay back and be perfect."[13]

Part of being perfect involves appearance. The message that immigrant women get from their adopted country is to be thin. Karen Hough, a middle school counselor from Virginia, hears her Latino students discuss this often. She has started a group to talk with immigrant students about their body image. She explains:

> It's hard enough at their age anyway. But when they are starting to go through an identity crisis and they feel that they don't fit in, you hear them saying things like they hate how they look. You have to tell them that what is acceptable in America is not always right [for them].[14]

Myths and Misconceptions

Statistics show that 12 million to 13 million Americans have eating disorders. Ninety percent are women, and 6 to 15 percent will die from their disorders.[15] These facts are only part of the picture. Eating disorders are surrounded by many myths and misconceptions.

Some of the most widely spread myths serve to disguise the problem. For example, many people believe that anorexics do not eat at all. They also think that anorexia is incurable. It is also a common misconception that all anorexics are thin and emaciated.[16]

Anorexics and bulimics are masters at hiding their problem and their bodies. They often view themselves as overweight or "big" even when they are already underweight. Even when norexics continue to feel hunger, they deny themselves all but very small quantities of food Many dress in layers to cover obvious weight loss. Many are not losing weight but are abusing their bodies by restricting themselves to unnaturally small portions or unhealthy foods—a diet of nothing but ice cream, for example.

Another common myth is that men do not suffer from eating disorders. Although the percentage of males is much lower, men do have the same problems as women and for similar reasons, such as low self-esteem and striving to be perfect. And they are less likely to seek help to overcome their disorder.

Dr. Thomas Holbrook began his obsession with food and exercise after an injury forced him to stop running his usual fifteen miles a day. He says, "I started weighing myself every day, and even though I was not gaining weight, I started feeling fatter. For the next twelve years, I did everything I could to rid my body of 'the fat.'"[17]

Dr. Holbrook began walking up to six hours a day and often survived on rice cakes for lunch. He attributes his body-image problem to male stereotypes he was exposed to while growing up: "I grew up in the era of Charles Atlas and superheroes, and soldiers, and all the mystique of the strong, courageous man," he says. "It may appear in a somewhat different form now, but I think that it is still

Exercise is essential for health, but over-exercising can be related to an eating disorder.

a prized stereotype, and I think that has a tremendous impact on vulnerable people."[18]

He also believes he used food control to help him cope with an alcoholic father and an emotionally unpredictable mother.

There are many similarities among men and women with eating disorders. Both sexes may also suffer from depression, anxiety, alcohol or drug abuse, or other psychiatric conditions. Most have distorted body images—they see themselves as fat even if they are not. One difference is that because men begin puberty later, they also exhibit signs of eating disorders at a later age, on average, such as fifteen or sixteen, rather than age thirteen or even younger, as girls do.[19]

Effects and Dangers

The effects of anorexia and bulimia are multiple and potentially fatal. Continual purging causes erosion of the teeth due to the acid content of vomit. It can also result in severe gum disease, cavities, and tooth loss. Vomiting can also lead to tearing and bleeding of the esophagus and the formation of hiatal hernias, which create heartburn.[20]

Laxative and diuretic abuse can cause cramping, nausea, and bloating. Abnormal changes in the colon and bowel disease can occur, as well as the development of ulcers.[21]

Due to poor nutrition, anorexics experience feelings of anxiety as their blood sugar levels drop. Undernourishment experienced by both anorexics and bulimics can also result in amenorrhea (the stopping of menstruation). Women with this condition are also at risk of osteoporosis, a disease in which bones become less dense and more likely to fracture. This condition is a major health threat to older women, but younger females can also experience it.[22]

Another serious risk to those with eating disorders is cardiac (heart) complications. They often have irregular or slow heartbeats and low blood pressure. There can be thinning of the heart muscle wall itself. Sudden cardiac arrest and death can occur. Karen Carpenter, a famous singer who battled anorexia and bulimia, died this way.[23]

At Risk

There are signs that may indicate that someone is at risk for developing an eating disorder. Spending a lot of time on grooming and worrying excessively about appearance is one indicator. Dieting in order to change one's appearance can also be a sign. Using food or exercise to relieve anxiety or depression may denote a problem. Being compulsive about food or exercise or even extreme behavior in other areas of life can indicate that a person is at risk for eating disorders.[24]

One defense against development of eating disorders is to educate young children about proper nutrition. Everyone needs a varied diet, including protein, fruits, and vegetables, but some sweets and fats are all right too. Experts say the key is moderation. It is fine to eat pizza, but a slice or two rather than the whole pie. Eating cookies is fine, but not a whole bag.

Judy Scheel, a social worker who directs an eating-disorder clinic, emphasizes balance in all areas. "I don't think people realize the impact of what we say to our children," she says. "We need to develop healthy self-esteem in our children, and encourage balanced meals, as well as balanced emotions."[25]

People with eating disorders need professional help. Traditional psychotherapy involving the entire family is the route usually suggested by experts. One newer therapy has the family take charge of feeding the patient as though he or she were starving for some other medical reason. Recovery is difficult, and many patients experience relapse. Some experts say it can take up to seven years to fully recover. Dr. James Lock, a child psychiatrist studying new treatments at Stanford, makes a very important point. He says, "No single treatment is going to work for everybody."[26]

Professional therapy and sometimes even hospitalization are recommended treatments. Those with eating disorders who try to cure themselves without professional treatment face very low odds of success.

Self-Mutilation:
A Cry for Help

Mary, a thirteen-year-old girl, is a cutter. She deliberately injures herself, slicing wounds into her arms and legs with razors and knives. When she first began hurting herself, she barely scratched the surface of her skin. That behavior changed. Mary remembers, "I started to get really deep. The more blood I saw, the more relief I felt."[1]

She explains that the act of cutting herself relieves stress: "I would just watch it bleed. It's hard to explain, so just bear with me. I guess it just felt like a stress reliever—I was getting the emotional pain out with the physical pain."[2]

Mary was sexually molested at the age of eight. Her parents put her into therapy to help her deal with the horrible episode. They thought Mary had recovered well. She had many friends and was class valedictorian. They had no idea that Mary was still suffering and had turned to self-injuring. They were alerted by a phone call from Mary's therapist. Mary had e-mailed her confessing that she had been drinking and cutting herself.

The practice of self-injuring is more common than most people realize. A study by Karen Conterio and Dr. Wendy Lader, the founders of SAFE (Self-Abuse Finally Ends) in Chicago, Illinois, reports about one percent of the population is likely to self-injure; most are female.[3]

B. J. Thom, executive director of SAFE Canada and a recovered self-cutter, says she has treated cutters as young as six years old. Thom also emphasizes anyone might turn to self-injuring when under pressure. "It has no financial, ethnic, or social boundaries. We all do it to handle crisis and stresses in our life."[4]

This dangerous practice gained wide public notice after Princess Diana admitted during an interview that she deliberately cut her arms and legs during her unhappy marriage. She revealed her reasons, saying, "You have so much pain inside yourself that you try and hurt yourself on the outside because you want help."[5]

A Growing Phenomenon

Self-injuring is most often expressed by cutting, but burning the skin, biting, and pulling hair out can also take place. The journal *Pediatric News* reports that self-cutting is almost epidemic among adolescents. The behavior occurs among those who are mentally healthy as well as those with various mental illnesses, such as borderline personality disorder, major depression, obsessive-compulsive disorder, post-traumatic stress disorder, and various types of psychosis.[6] When a person is psychotic, he or she is out of touch with reality and is severely disturbed mentally. Some cutters may be psychotic only during cutting episodes.[7] Like other addictive behaviors, self-mutilation is self-reinforcing; that is, doing it makes the person want to do it more. In addition, the intensity and frequency must increase for the desired effect of relief to be achieved.[8]

The disorder is often hidden well by the self-cutter. And self-cutters can do well in school and society. Those around them may never know they have a problem. Lindsey, a fifteen-year-old high school junior, is a perfect example. She vividly describes the double life she lives:

> *If you met me you'd never know I'm a cutter. If I were to list my mental problems on one side—eating disorder, self-mutilation, major depression, two suicide attempts—and my credentials on the other side—honors student, first place in the school poetry contest, and award for most school spirit—it doesn't look like it could be the same person. But it's me. I'm a good actress, I can act so happy. I just want people to understand that I'm not crazy and I'm not a freak, I'm just scared and sad and alone. It doesn't matter what anyone else does or says or thinks when you see nothing in the mirror.[9]*

One common misconception about self-injuring is that a self-cutting episode is, in fact, a suicide attempt. Steven Levenkron, a New York psychotherapist who treats cutters, adamantly opposes this view. He believes some therapists wrongly think their cutting patients may kill themselves. "But this is not a suicide attempt," he says. "They all assume they will live to cut again."[10] He notes the cuts are generally less than an inch long and are not life threatening.

Self-cutting may actually have antisuicidal benefits. One woman explains how cutting helps her deal with her feelings of helplessness and avoid suicide: "[I hurt myself] as a way not to kill myself."[11]

Natural Endorphins

Cutting can work as both a downer and an upper. Cutting numbs painful feelings and provides a sense of disassociation or detachment. This is described over and over again by cutters who are victims of sexual abuse. During cutting episodes they "escape" painful memories and release pent-up anger.[12]

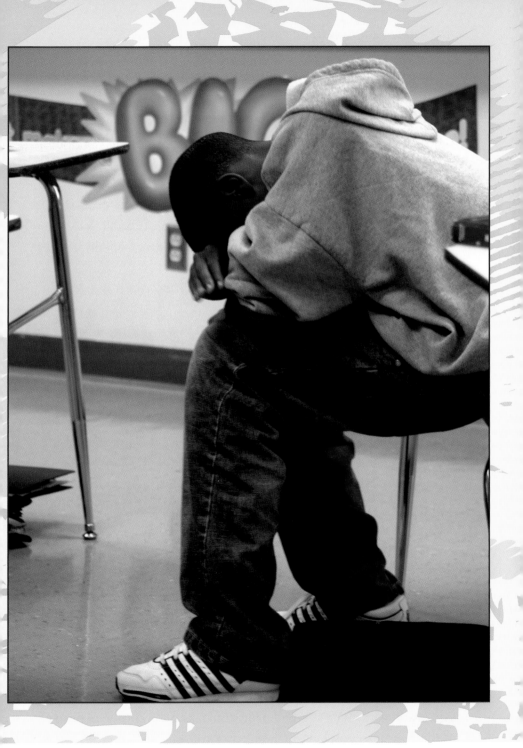

Self-injury can be related to depression, but experts say it is not the same as a suicide attempt.

On the other hand, cutters who are depressed or numb say they experience feelings of life and stimulation when they injure themselves and see the blood. How does this happen?

It is an effect of hormones in the body called endorphins. When the body is injured, endorphins are naturally released. They are designed to fight anxiety, agitation, and depression. Cutters gain temporary control over their emotions by this natural occurrence. They can forget their trauma and focus on the pleasurable sensation of release. Cutters are using the body's natural "drug" of endorphins to alter their mood.[13]

Additionally, cutting brings notice to self-injurers. Like children who misbehave in order to draw focus to themselves even at the risk of punishment, some cutters are using their actions to get help and attention.[14]

Those who self-mutilate have many reasons for their actions. Sexual abuse, severe trauma, or a painful loss is often a factor. They remain tormented by these experiences and emotions. Many—like Princess Diana, who had eating disorders—are victims of multiple disorders.

There are two distinct characteristics most self-injurers have. The first is a feeling of mental disintegration or an inability to think. The second is an intense rage, usually directed toward a powerful figure in their lives, often a parent.[15]

Self-injurers usually harm themselves with great care in an almost ceremonial fashion. Their cutting sessions are planned. Most take care to inflict wounds where they will not be easily seen and can be covered by clothing.

Lost Years

Elizabeth Francis was a high school senior when her ordeal with self-injuring began. Her sister had been raped, and the family focused all of their attention on helping her. "My sister was running the family," Elizabeth remembers. "It wasn't her fault, but there wasn't much left for me."[16]

Elizabeth was a talented gymnast. Concentrating on training with her coach was important to her. When her coach made the decision to return to Russia, she was devastated. Elizabeth gave up her sport and no longer had gymnastics as an outlet. Her family did not realize how upset she was.

"I was like an animal in a caged box that's trying to get out," she says. "That's pretty much what it felt like."[17]

Elizabeth began cutting herself when she was a senior in high school. She would use anything she could get her hands on to inflict the wounds—broken glass, staples, her own fingernails. She cut herself on her arms, belly, and hip—always on her left side.

Her mother noticed long gashes on her shoulder when Elizabeth was getting out of a shower. Her parents did not understand why she was harming herself. They sought therapy for Elizabeth. She was also diagnosed with an eating disorder and obsessive-compulsive disorder. After suffering for years, she found a therapist she liked and is recovering. But she admits it is not easy.

"I may not cut every day, but that urge will always be there. I know I'm going to be dealing with this for the rest of my life."[18]

The Male Perspective

A small percentage of self-injurers are male. Men who practice this are generally prone to injure themselves more severely than women.

Andrew, who began cutting himself at the age of nineteen, used kitchen knives to carve his skin. He later switched to safety razors so he would not lose too much blood. Sometimes, Andrew blacks out and has no memory of the act of cutting. He also uses sleeping pills and alcohol to numb his depression.

Andrew's troubles began early. He remembers trying to injure himself as a child. Between the ages of two and ten he would bang his head against the wall until he knocked himself unconscious.

He sees his self-cutting as a form of self-punishment. It also helps him vent his aggressive impulses. Andrew still suffers from the deaths of his grandmother and grandfather, both of whom died in his presence. He also feels a responsibility for his mother's fragile mental health.

Andrew describes the irrational and exaggerated fears that fuel his cutting episodes: "One of the central fears that comes up for me is that I might hurt or even kill other people, directly or indirectly, by what I say or do."[19]

He admits he has changed his behavior "from having to cut to wanting to cut."[20] Therapy is helping Andrew, but he still has a long way to go.

The Price They Pay

The SAFE program, which has been in existence for more than a dozen years, has treated thousands of cutters. SAFE reports that many patients have been hospitalized innumerable times for posing a danger to themselves. Many are on psychiatric disability—because of their mental problems, they are unable to hold down a job, and so they receive money from the government. Cutting has cost some patients their friends, family, housing, and any happiness they had.[21]

Karen Conterio feels the only way a cutter can recover is to make the decision to help themselves. She says:

> They chose to start doing this and they have to choose to stop. When someone says they feel like self-injuring we tell them, "No, you're thinking of self-injuring in response to a feeling." Breaking that down helps them master what's going on with them. Those who don't want to stop don't do very well in this program. They have too much of an investment in staying sick. Getting better means having to be responsible, get a job, get off disability.[22]

Dr. Tracy Alderman suggests that her patients learn to identify the triggers that make them want to self-injure and then find alternative options such as exercising, calling a friend, drawing with red marker on their skin, or holding an ice cube until the urge passes.[23]

Some therapists strongly feel that cutting should not be forbidden until other replacement skills are firmly in place. Alderman explains:

"I help reduce the frequency of self-injury only if that's what the patient wants. I encourage the patients to see self-injury as a behavior and a choice, not an illness or psychopathology, and to use it as long as necessary until they find something better to replace it."[24]

This goes along with the antisuicidal benefits of cutting that many patients express.

Those in the SAFE program do sign a no-harm contract. Dr. Wendy Lader, clinical director of the SAFE program, says, "We see this as the philosophy of empowerment—we want to speak to the healthy side of our patients."[25] Different treatment strategies should be explored for different patients. Structure and accountability do play a role in most therapies.

Being Ready to Stop

Being ready to stop is a crucial step in overcoming self-injuring. There are some criteria that may help determine if self-cutters are prepared to begin the difficult process of recovery:

- A solid emotional support system of friends and family is in place.

- They have at least two people available to call if they feel they want to hurt themselves.

- They feel comfortable talking about their problem with at least three different people.

- They have a list of ten things they can do instead of self-injuring.

- They have a place to go if they need to leave the house.

- They feel confident that they can get rid of all the things they might use to self-injure, such as knives and razors.

- They are willing to feel uncomfortable, scared, and frustrated as they recover.

- They feel confident that they can think about hurting themselves without actually doing so.

- They want to stop.[26]

The more of these points patients feel sure of, the higher their chance of success. Self-injuring is a frightening, dangerous, addictive behavior. It is hard for people to understand why anyone would do this to himself. Fortunately, professional help is available, and self-injury is being openly addressed in our society today.

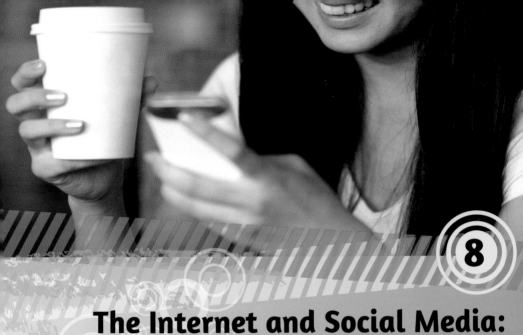

The Internet and Social Media: Obsession and Isolation

The Internet is growing at an astounding rate, as is the number of teens using it. A study by the U.S. government indicates that 2 million new users go on-line each month. Seventy-five percent of teens between the ages of fourteen to seventeen and 65 percent of those between the ages of ten to thirteen use the Internet regularly.[1] Some people think these figures indicate that teenagers are on-line too much and that they are at risk for Internet addiction. But is it a genuine addiction?

Dr. Ivan Goldberg, a New York psychiatrist, first used the term "Internet addiction" in 1995. The idea was met with controversy and disagreement but is now accepted as a legitimate disorder. Though the American Psychiatric Association does not at this point list Internet addiction in its manual of disorders, the American Psychological Association has recognized it as a mental health disorder since 1997. Many psychotherapists treat patients for Internet addiction.

Maressa Hecht Orzack, a clinical psychologist at Harvard Medical School, has treated such addicts for several years. She notes that most of her patients have at least one other problem: "Depression, social phobia, impulse control disorder, and attention deficit disorder are commonest. Several of my patients have a history of another addiction or of substance abuse. A few are bipolar, suicidal, or prone to violent outbreaks."[2]

She also points out that different people become Internet dependent for different reasons. "Some use it for excitement or a new sense of identity; some to reduce tension; some for companionship; others, most tellingly, because it's a place where they belong. Typically they are lonely people."[3]

Dr. David Greenfield, a psychologist, author, and director of the Center for Internet Studies in West Hartford, Connecticut, conducted an on-line survey and found that of those who responded, "Upwards of seventy percent admitted to losing track of time on-line and spending far more time than they intended. Over fifty percent use it to alter their mood."[4] Greenfield admits that Internet addiction is difficult to define and that the term "compulsive Internet use" may more accurately define the problem. He points out that there are numerous aspects of the Internet that can become compulsive and be a real problem for users, including chat rooms, e-mail, stock trading, pornography, and gambling.[5]

He says research has shown that when some people use the Internet, it causes their body to boost production of dopamine, a neurochemical that creates an intense sense of gratification. This surge of pleasure can help create an addiction.

Greenfield poses key questions to help determine if there is a problem: "Are you using the Internet on a regular basis to alter your mood? Do you intentionally use the Internet to escape or avoid real-life situations? Is your use altering or impacting your life negatively in any way, shape, or form?"[6]

Avoidance and Isolation

Becky was sixteen years old when her life began to change. Her parents got a divorce, and she immersed herself in the world of the Internet. She spent hours in chat rooms talking to other teens who were going through the same experience. She felt she could really connect with them and was free to express her true emotions without fear of rejection.

Soon she was spending more time with her on-line friends than with her school friends. She began to fail three of her classes. Her mother threatened to take the computer away, but Becky persuaded her not to. Then her mother began dating and convinced herself that Becky's time on the computer was a good thing, since it made up for her mother's absence. Soon, Becky began faking illness to stay home and chat on-line. Her Internet use was out of control.

By her senior year, her schoolwork was so bad that she was in danger of not graduating. Her mother contacted a mental health counselor, and with help, Becky graduated. She was given a laptop computer as a reward. She returned to her old habits. Her excessive Internet use put her in danger of failing her first semester of college. Becky is back in therapy trying to turn her life around.[7]

Unsupervised

Another troubling factor concerning teens and the Internet is inappropriate material. Thousands of teens surf the Internet unsupervised and visit sites featuring pornography and other objectionable subjects. Parents cannot monitor their Internet use every hour of the day.

Some parents turn to specialized computer software for help. Filtering and blocking software is designed to screen out unwanted material and prevent it from appearing on the computer. Sometimes the software even shuts the computer off if a user tries to access objectionable Web sites. Monitoring software leaves an audit trail showing exactly which sites were visited, enabling parents to track their child's choices.

Schools and libraries often use filters to keep inappropriate material away from children, but sometimes this prevents users from accessing legitimate educational sites as well.

These options do offer some protection, but they are not foolproof. Kids who are adept at computer skills can often bypass the blocks and access whatever they wish.[8]

One mother purchased filtering software for her home computer but ran into a perplexing problem. Her fifteen-year-old son had installed a secret password on the computer. She could not even turn it on to install the new software. She was stunned to realize he had shut her out of that part of his life completely.[9]

Kathryn Montgomery of the Center for Media Education comments, "The nature of the Internet is that it separates children from their families."[10] She also feels there is a gap between knowledge and experience that poses a danger to teens. She says, "The next generation is entering into a world in many ways they'll be very tech savvy in, but in other ways they are not necessarily mature enough to navigate that world."[11]

There is also the problem of computers being accessed by teens in school and public libraries. Software that monitors or blocks objectionable material has some drawbacks. Certain phrases or key words that restrict usage may very well block legitimate and helpful material. Those who favor blocks claim that they work. A recent study by the Kaiser Family Foundation concluded: "The Internet filters most frequently used by schools and libraries can effectively block pornography without significantly impeding access to on-line health information, but only if they aren't set at their most restrictive levels."[12]

Many of those who oppose censorship and support free speech do not favor filters. Parental and public restrictions as well as filtering and blocking software can all be beneficial in monitoring young people on-line. But the systems are not perfect, and personal freedoms can be compromised.

Chat Rooms

Chat rooms enjoy a huge popularity among teens but can be very dangerous. These are places where people can speak freely in cyberspace, sometimes trying on different personalities. Chat rooms provide an instant sense of belonging and of anonymity. This same sense of secrecy and freedom is what draws pedophiles and predators to use chat rooms to their own advantage. They meet unsuspecting young people on-line and sometimes try to lure them to meet them in person.

Christina Long was an altar girl and co-captain of the cheerleading squad at her Roman Catholic school. The thirteen-year-old girl also had a big secret. She had developed her own personal, sexy Web site and was using chat rooms to exchange racy messages with adult men. She would sometimes meet them for sex.

She agreed to see one twenty-five-year-old man at a mall. They had sex in the parking lot, then he strangled Christina and dumped her body in a ravine. Christina's death was the second case of a child's homicide attributed directly to an Internet meeting.[13]

Watchdog groups report that the number of Internet predators is growing. Documented cases of child abusers who go on-line to lure kids into personal meetings have soared. In the mid-1990s the number was around one hundred; it is now up to approximately four thousand per year. One study found that 12 percent of the kids approached go through with an actual meeting. The potential danger is staggering.[14]

"Cam Girls" and "Cam Boys"

There is a new craze of "cam boys" and "cam girls" who use their own Web sites to publish personal diaries, exchange e-mail, and publish snapshots and even videos of themselves. Some of these sites get up to five thousand hits per day and one hundred to two hundred e-mails, many asking the teens to take off their clothes or perform sexual acts. The teens do not necessarily honor those requests, but it does not stop them from continuing their sites. Most do not feel there is anything wrong with their on-line activity.

One fifteen-year-old girl named Nay, who is from an upper-middle-class family, admits, "It's kind of exciting to get all this attention. I've met a lot of cool people. They give me advice and I give them advice. We're all strangers, but in a way we're all friends, too."[15]

Nay's mother, Barbara, is well aware of her daughter's activities and has mixed feelings. But, she admits, she feels it is safer to flirt on-line than at the mall as she did when she was a teen.

Nay also included a wish list on her site of items she wants—and her "fans" started sending them to her. She recently received a silver cordless phone.

She insists that hearing praise about how well designed her Web page is has helped her self-confidence. She also says she received two computer job offers but turned them down because of her age. Nay says, "It has really boosted my self-esteem, not to the point where I'm conceited, where I'm all superior, but to the point where I'm a happy teenage girl."[16]

Zakh, a sixteen-year-old "cam" boy, actively posts his journal on his Web site. He also corresponds with many fans. He eagerly accepts gifts, insisting it is a mutually beneficial arrangement. He claims the adults who write to him are lonely, and he makes them happy by talking to them. "Basically, if you want anything, these people will get it for you," he says.[17] He lists a DVD player, sixty-two compact discs, and eighteen movies as among the gifts he has received.

He knows that some of the people who send him things fantasize about having sex with him, but he does not let it bother him. Zakh just tells himself, "Free DVD, free DVD."[18]

Cyber Cafes

Cyber cafes are another source of controversy. In larger cities, these cafes usually stay open until 2:00 A.M., and many teens spend several hours in them daily. It is a social hangout that gives them a chance to get away from home and to be with others who share their interests. Most young people use cyber cafes as a low-cost pastime (about two dollars per hour to be on-line). Linked to other computers, they play games, testing their skills against players around the world.

Calvin Williams is a nineteen-year-old fan of *Counter-Strike,* a cyber game in which terrorists garner points by blowing each other away. He says his favorite cyber cafe is "my second home."[19] He spends about ten hours a day on-line.

Authorities are not as happy about the existence of the cafes. They say city curfews are not being enforced and the cafes are a magnet for troubled teens.[20] One dispute that erupted between gamers resulted in a fight with baseball bats.

A month later, outside the same location, a twenty-year-old was stabbed to death. The customers inside were unaware of the murder. Officer Tim Kovacs was there and remembers: "Not only were they oblivious, they continued to play after they were told. They seem more annoyed by the inconvenience."[21]

Internet Addiction as a Defense

Michael Ian Campbell was an eighteen-year-old high school graduate when his Internet activity nearly destroyed his world. He sent a message through an on-line chat room to Erin Walton, a Columbine High School student who had lived through the horrible massacre. She was a sophomore when two students shot and killed thirteen people before killing themselves. Michael threatened to finish the violence that had begun with the shooting spree.[22] She told officials about the threat, and her school was closed for two days as a precaution.

Campbell was charged by a federal grand jury for making a threat across state lines. He was freed on one hundred thousand dollars bail and issued an apology stating, "I am horrified at what I have done and its consequences. I did not really understand what you in Colorado had gone through."[23]

His lawyer mounted an unusual defense, claiming that Campbell was not guilty and had acted while immersed in the virtual world of the Internet. He claimed that Campbell had made a virtual threat, not one made with a "criminal state of mind."[24]

Michael Campbell later changed his plea to guilty, and his lawyer argued for probation. Campbell was given a four-month prison sentence and was ordered not to use the Internet for three years following his release. Many felt this was a mere slap on the wrist, considering the seriousness of his threat. If the case had gone to trial, would Campbell's Internet addiction have been a strong argument in his defense? Many law professionals do not think so. Law professor April Major points out that proving his actions were involuntary would be difficult: "You're pointing and clicking or you're writing in a chat room or something like that. So proving that there's some type of involuntary nature about it is going to be tough."[25]

Too Much Internet?

How can teens and concerned parents agree on what is proper use of the Internet? Conditions vary depending on the age of the teen. Some suggested guidelines include time limits on use, teens not having their own passwords, access only to safe chat rooms, no unsupervised use, and agreeing to stick to set limitations.[26]

What are some signs an Internet addiction may be present? It may help to ask the following questions:

- Is there a preoccupation with the Internet?
- Is the Internet being used for increasing amounts of time?
- Is Internet use out of control?
- Are there feelings of restlessness or irritability when Internet use is denied?
- Is the Internet being used to escape bad moods?
- Is Internet use being hidden or denied?
- Does on-line time extend longer than intended?
- Are on-line fees excessive?[27]

Computers are an important part of teens' lives, but overuse of the Internet can cause social and emotional problems.

Helping Internet addicts can be difficult. The first step is usually intervention; the addict must be confronted about the problem. Recovery involves treatment and monitoring and restricting computer use. Recovery rates can be poor, since monitoring is difficult. Vaughn J. Howland, a social worker who organizes intervention sessions, feels even limited use for an addict in recovery is a mistake. His frustration is evident by his comment, "I'd like to put a bullet through the screen."[28]

On the other hand, Maressa Hecht Orzack compares Internet addiction to an eating disorder: "You can't always tell people to abstain. People have to deal with eating three meals a day, and they have to deal with work that must be done on a computer."[29]

Computers are a part of modern society. Compulsive behavior stemming from their use must be recognized and dealt with.

Social Media, Texting, and Sexting

The Facebook phenomenon has pushed Internet usage among teens to new levels. Since its inception in 2004, Facebook has steadily gained popularity, by some estimates reaching an incredible one billion users. Members create personal profiles and contact each other with updates, messages and by sharing pictures or Internet links. Facebook can also be accessed using smart phones and other mobile devices.

Many studies indicate that people are obsessed with Facebook and 48 percent say they update their profile during the night or as soon as they wake up. Dr. Larry Rosen, a professor of psychology at California State University, says that while using Facebook does not create psychological disorders, social networking sites can draw out negative emotional behaviors and aggressive tendencies. "If you already have narcissistic tendencies, these 'behind the screen' media will bring them out since you are not directly talking to people, only a screen."[30]

Researchers in Norway have developed a new scale to determine Facebook addiction. The Bergen Facebook Addiction Scale was tested on a group of 423 students in the form of a questionnaire. Results indicate that people who are anxious and socially insecure gravitate to Facebook and that females are more at risk of developing an addiction possibly because of the social aspect of Facebook.[31] All findings remain controversial and the argument has been made that research cannot keep up with electronic media. Ease of usage and ways available to connect to social media change quickly.

Texting is an excellent case in point. Its popularity is remarkable. Teens text dozens if not hundreds of times per day. While this behavior can be merely time consuming, annoying or rude, when practiced in a moving vehicle it can be deadly. Seventy-three percent of texting teens ages sixteen to seventeen have been in a car when the driver was texting.[32]

A study conducted by UK Transport Research Laboratory found that drivers who text are significantly more impaired than ones who drive drunk. While texting, drivers reaction times deteriorated by 35 percent with a decrease of 91 percent in steering ability. This compares to drunken driving reaction times diminishing by 12 percent.[33] Statistics such as these are causing many states to enact no texting while driving laws.

Cell phones present another dangerous activity to teens—sexting. This practice may feed other risky behaviors. Studies show that teens who send elicit messages and pictures to others may be more likely to be sexually active. Jeff Temple, a psychologist who worked on a study with teens in a Houston, Texas high school, found that girls were particularly vulnerable. Girls who sent naked photos of themselves were more likely to engage in risky sex, to have had multiple recent sex partners and to use drugs or alcohol before sex. Temple says, "What they're doing in their off-line lives is what they're doing in their on-line lives."[34]

Legal problems also plague teens who engage in sexting. Phillip Alpert was eighteen years old when he had an argument with his longtime sixteen-year-old girlfriend. In retaliation he sent a naked photo of her to dozens of her friends and family. "It was a stupid thing I did because I was upset and tired and it was the middle of the night and I was an immature kid," said Alpert.[35]

Alpert was arrested and charged with sending child pornography. Ultimately, he was sentenced to five years probation and required to register as a sex offender until he reaches the age of forty three. Because of sexting, Alpert is a convicted felon.

Jesse Logan, an eighteen-year-old young woman from Ohio, paid the ultimate price due to sexting. She had sent nude pictures of herself to her boyfriend and after their breakup he sent them to other high school girls. Jesse was called names and taunted so severely she was afraid to go to school. She shared her story on a local television show stating, "I just want to make sure no one else will have to go through this again."[36]

Two months after the interview, Jesse hanged herself in her bedroom. Her grieving mother, Cynthia Logan, now shares her daughter's story in hopes spreading awareness of the dangers of sexting. "She was being tortured," says Logan. "I'm trying my best to get the message out there."[37]

What Can Help

Teens seem to be at risk for addictions for many reasons. Lack of maturity, peer pressure, and poor coping skills, combined with a natural desire to rebel, can easily send a teen spiraling into serious problems. Unfortunately, some teens lack parental support and guidance to help them get through troubled times. Education is also a key component for prevention. If teens do not realize the dangers of addiction, they have no incentive to avoid it.

Programs such as DARE (Drug Abuse Resistance Education) are one way of educating young people. DARE provides information by bringing police officers into schools to talk about drugs. The program is used in 80 percent of the country's school districts, most of the time only in elementary school. Only 25 percent of districts offer it in middle school, and only 10 percent offer it in high school. DARE's antidrug message seems to be falling short. The program has also been criticized for its use of lecturing. A study has been conducted to find ways of improving DARE's mission. The program is being revamped to encourage more student interaction. For example, teens might be encouraged to discuss how they would react at a party where kids were drinking. The new DARE is being tested on thirty-five thousand students in two hundred schools.[1]

Zili Sloboda, an investigator on the DARE study, applauds the changes. "It has to be highly interactive," she says. "Children have to be able to try it on in their own lives."[2]

But schools cannot tackle the problem alone. Parental support remains the best defense against kids falling into an addiction trap. Many parents struggle to survive and are not available to be with their kids. The increase in single-parent families compounds the problem. The number of households headed by one parent raising children alone has risen to 9.8 million.[3] Currently, the average adolescent has at least forty hours per week of unsupervised time.[4] For many teens, this is more than enough time to get into trouble.

Dr. Robert Blum, a researcher at the University of Minnesota who conducted a study of teens, indicates that his findings place a good part of the blame on parents and society. "We call ourselves a family-oriented society—we are not," he says. "We are a work-oriented society." He noted that many children after school "are left to their own devices. Kids need structure to grow. Are we, as parents, willing to invest in our kids?"[5]

In many households, both parents need to work to pay living expenses. They have no other option. Most communities have few, if any, structured after-school programs geared to helping older children and teens. There are few adult role models to mentor those in need.

And in fact, teens want to spend more time with adults. Lynn McDonald, a psychologist at the University of Wisconsin's School of Education, reports, "This is the surprise: Youth are [saying], 'I want to talk to an adult, but people are zipping by us.' What's interesting is that this research is coming out just as adults are not around."[6]

Poll after poll turns up evidence of the importance of parents in a teen's life. Twenty-one percent of teens age twelve to fifteen listed spending more time with family as their biggest concern. This was the top response in a survey conducted by the YMCA.[7]

A Family Policy

Teens need to be open with their parents about their feelings and their needs. Sometimes, honest discussion and an actual family policy on drugs and other dangerous behaviors can help. Having the rules and punishments down in writing helps to avoid misunderstandings. If teens are part of the formation of the guidelines, they may be more willing to adhere to them.

It also helps for teens to be willing to introduce their friends to their parents and to tell parents about their plans and activities. If a mutual pattern of trust can be established, the relationship between parents and teens can be strengthened.

A study from the Baylor College of Medicine in Houston found that kids who do not feel connected to their families will intentionally distance themselves and be more open to risky behavior. Kids who maintain a good relationship with those at home will be less likely to engage in substance abuse. James H. Bray, coauthor of the study, says, "Monitoring your child's activities shows that you care. But there's a big difference between that and controlling your kid, which can be suffocating and spark the rebellious behavior that leads to substance abuse."[8]

No Quick Fixes

Behavioral and chemically based addictions have similar effects. The addiction must be repeated over and over and in increasing doses to obtain the high the addict craves. It is a progressive syndrome and one of the most costly public health problems in the United States.

Many addicts need professional help to overcome their problems. This care can easily cost thousands of dollars. Insurance restrictions can, in some cases, stop the care before the addict is fully rehabilitated. Skyrocketing health-care costs are a continuing problem in this country, with no solution in sight.

Alcoholics Anonymous is the most well-known treatment organization in the world. Its twelve-step program of rehabilitation has had much success. It involves many basic principles, including examining one's lifestyle, being accountable for one's actions, and having the willingness to make amends and make the changes

Family involvement can help teens stay out of the addiction trap.

necessary to improve. These steps have been modified and used by many other recovery programs dealing with all types of addictions. Most often, regular group meetings take place, and members have a sponsor or support buddy to call if they feel they need help.[9]

Support from family and friends is crucial. Most addicts are incapable of handling their problems alone. Understanding and open communication between all parties concerned is helpful. There are no quick fixes.

Education and knowledge are key factors to prevention. There are countless organizations working to help people overcome every conceivable type of addiction. Most of these can be found through Internet searches or by referral from a health-care or school professional. Taking the first step can be difficult, but there is hope. Teens can avoid the sad, difficult, and dangerous life of an addict.

Chapter Notes

Chapter 1. The Addiction Risk

1. Jon Gallo, "Remembering Damien," *The Washington Post*, June 29, 2000.

2. Ibid.

3. Ibid.

4. U.S. Department of Health and Human Services, *Don't Harm Yourself*, December 4, 2000.

5. Tara Parker-Pope, "Helping Kids Deal With Stresses of Life May Be Most Effective Antidrug Strategy," *The Wall Street Journal*, May 21, 2002.

6. Peter Grier, "The Parent Trap: No Teen Time," *The Christian Science Monitor*, April 25, 2000.

7. Ibid.

8. Carolyn Costin, *Your Dieting Daughter, Is She Dying for Attention?* (New York: Brunner/Mazel, 1997), p. 54.

9. Ibid., p. 99.

10. Carl Sherman, "Today's Self-mutilators are Younger, Healthier," *Clinical Psychiatry News*, May 2002, p. 38.

11. Ibid.

12. Horacio Sierra, "Caught in the Web," *The Miami Herald*, February 23, 2000.

13. Ibid.

14. Ibid.

15. University of Michigan C.S. Mott Children's Hospital National Poll on Children's Health, "For Youth Sexting: Public Supports Education, Not Criminal Charges," *U.S. Newswire*, Ann Arbor, MI: March 20, 2012.

Chapter 2.   Drugs: Types and Dangers

1. Peggy Brown, "Too Much for Your Brain?: The Effects of Ecstasy are Anything But Ecstasy," *Newsday*, March 19, 2001.

2. Ibid.

3. Gary L. Somdahl, *Drugs and Kids* (Salem, Ore.: Dimi Press, 1996), p. 85.

4. Ibid., p. 86.

5. Ibid., p. 88.

6. Ibid., p. 89.

7. Nikki Babbit, *Adolescent Drug and Alcohol Abuse* (Sebastopol, Calif.: O'Reilly, 2000), p. 32.

8. Patrik Jonsson, "Drugs Becoming a Rarer Sight in Schools," *The Christian Science Monitor*, August 21, 2002.

9. Ibid.

10. "The Agony of Ecstasy," *The Wall Street Journal*, October 15, 2002.

11. Svetlana Kolchik, "Parents Are Unaware of Ecstasy Risk," *USA Today*, October 21, 2002

12. "The Agony of Ecstasy."

13. Ellen Creager, "In Ecstasy's Shadow," *Miami Herald*, April 16, 2001.

14. Ibid.

15. Ibid.

16. Jamie Stockwell, "Teens Turning to Ecstasy," *The Washington Post*, October 4, 2001.

17. Kolchik.

18. Geoff Boucher, "Lawmakers Targeting the Ecstasy of Raves," *The Los Angeles Times*, August 3, 2002.

19. Creager.

20. Clinician Publishing Group, "Medicinal Marijuana," *Clinician Reviews*, April 2000.

21. Ibid.

22. Robert Patrick, "Annual Teen Drug Study Finds Mixed Results," *The Los Angeles Times*, August 21, 2002.

23. "Parents Warned on Pot's Toll," *The Los Angeles Times*, September 18, 2002.

24. Ibid.

25. John P. Walters, "The Myth of 'Harmless' Marijuana," *The Washington Post*, May 1, 2002.

26. Raychelle Cassada Lohmann, "Bath Salts—the New Designer Drug," *Psychology Today*, June 13, 2012, <http://www.psychologytoday.com/print/98355> (October 27, 2012).

27. Synthetic Drug Use is on a Dramatic Rise, Including Bath Salts," *American College of Emergency Physicians*, <http://www.emergencycareforyou.org/YourHealth/InjuryPrevention/Default.aspx?id=1916> October 28, 2012.

28. Kevin Dolak, "Bath Salts: Use of Dangerous Drug Increasing Across the U.S.," *ABC NEWS.go.com*, June 5, 2012, <http://abcnews.go.com/Health/bath-salts-dangerous-drug-increasing-us/story?id=16496076#.UI273mc9iTa> (October 27, 2012.)

29. "Synthetic Drug Use is on a Dramatic Rise, Including Bath Salts," *American College of Emergency Physicians*, <http://www.emergencycareforyou.org/YourHealth/InjuryPrevention/Default.aspx?id=1916> October 28, 2012.

30. Associated Press, "SC Coroner: Synthetic Pot Killed College Athlete," October 16, 2011, <http://aol.sportingnews.com/ncaa-basketball/story/2011-10-16/sc-coroner-synthetic-pot-killed-college-athlete> (October 28, 2012).

31. Mark Sappenfield, "New Laws Curb Teen Sport Drugs," *The Christian Science Monitor*, June 24, 2002.

32. Ibid.

33. Ibid.

34. Holcomb B. Noble, "Steroid Use by Teen-Age Girls Is Rising," *The New York Times*, June 1, 1999.

35. Ibid.

36. Babbit, p. 45.

37. Ibid., p. 15.

38. Ibid., p. 9.

Chapter 3. **Alcohol: The Drug of Choice**

1. Vigilance on Teen Drinking," *The Los Angeles Times,* May 20, 2001.

2. Robert Wallace, "'Tween 12 and 20," *The Mansfield (Ohio) News Journal,* November 22, 2002.

3. Brian Good, "Alcohol Update," *Men's Health,* September 2001.

4. "Alcohol: What You Don't Know Can Harm You," *College Drinking: Changing the Culture,* 2002, <http://www.collegedrinkingprevention.gov/ facts/alcohol.aspx> (July 27, 2005).

5. "Stats and Resources," *MADD,* n.d., <http://www.madd.org/stats/0,1056,1112,00.html> (June 14, 2005).

6. "Vigilance on Teen Drinking."

7. Ibid.

8. America's No. 1 Youth Drug Problem . . . Alcohol," *MADD,* Fall 2000, <http://www.madd.org/news/0,1056,1159,00.html> (March 30, 2004).

9. Ibid.

10. Ibid.

11. Ibid.

12. "In the Name of Love: Laws Named for Victims," *MADD,* 2001, <http://www.madd.org/news/0,1056,4321,00.html> (March 30, 2004).

13. Helen Rumbelow, "Alcohol Ads Often Reach Teens," *The Washington Post,* September 24, 2002.

14. Ibid.

15. Ibid.

16. Ibid.

17. The Associated Press, "Study: Children see more commercials for beer than for sneakers, gum or jeans," *The Mansfield (Ohio) News Journal,* December 18, 2002.

18. Shelly Branch, "Liquor Industry Is on Defensive After Study of Underage Drinking," *The Wall Street Journal,* February 27, 2002.

19. Ibid.

20. Ibid.

21. Ibid.

22. Patrick Welsh, "The Party Line: Even Good Parents Don't Know the Half of It," *The Washington Post*, March 4, 2001.

23. Ibid.

24. Laura Sessions Stepp, "The Parental Lines on Teens and Alcohol," *The Washington Post*, June 2, 2001.

25. Ibid.

26. Ibid.

27. Ibid.

28. Marilyn Gardner, "When Teens Drink, Parents May Pay," *The Christian Science Monitor*, September 6, 2000.

29. Jenn Abelson, "Alcohol-related deaths inspire prosecution of underage hosts," *Boston Globe*, December 28, 2003.

30. Ibid.

31. Ibid.

32. Brenden January, "Saliva Alcohol Testing vs. Teens' Rights," *The Washington Post*, February 2, 2001.

33. Ibid.

Chapter 4. Inhalant Abuse: The Silent Epidemic

1. "'Huffing': A Continuing Worry," *Child Health Alert*, May 1999.

2. Ibid.

3. United Press International, "Brain Images Show Damage From Inhalants," April 15, 2002.

4. Ibid.

5. Kathleen Fackelmann, "Millions of U.S. Kids Have Tried Huffing," *USA Today*, March 14, 2002.

6. David Haldane and Louise Roug, "Boy, 12, Dies After Sniffing Aerosol," *The Los Angeles Times*, March 21, 2000.

7. Ibid.

8. Ibid.

9. Kathleen Fackelmann, "Inhalants' Hidden Threat," *USA Today*, June 25, 2002.

10. Alive & Free, Education, *Awareness Is Key to Preventing Inhalant Abuse*, March 13, 2000.

11. Fackelmann.

12. Andrea Fine, "Getting High From a Can," *The Christian Science Monitor*, March 10, 1999.

13. Alive & Free.

14. Fackelmann.

15. Fine.

16. Ibid.

17. Michael Amon, "Huffing Blamed in Teen's Death," *The Washington Post*, March 22, 2002.

18. Ibid.

19. Ibid.

20. Ibid.

21. Alive & Free.

22. Amy Bracken, "Anti-Huffing Programs Work, Then Get Cut," *Youth Today*, April 2000.

23. Ibid.

24. United Press International.

Chapter 5. Smoking. Not Just a Bad Habit

1. Patricia J. Murphy, "Teen Smokers Tell Their Tales," *Current Health*, November 1999.

2. Ibid.

3. Ibid.

4. Ibid.

5. Ibid.

6. Thomas H. Maugh II, "Teens' Tobacco Addiction Faster Than Once Thought," *The Los Angeles Times*, August 29, 2002.

7. Ibid.

8. Eric F. Wagner, PhD, ed., *Nicotine Addiction Among Adolescents* (New York: Haworth Press, 2000), p. 30.

9. Michael Mannion, *How to Help Your Teenager Stop Smoking* (New York: Welcome Rain, 1999), p. 164.

10. Maugh.

11. Diana Zuckerman, "Smoking and Girls: A Deadly Mix," *Youth Today*, September 2001.

12. Ibid.

13. Dr. Paul Donohue, "Medical Advice," *The Mansfield (Ohio) News Journal*, July 20, 2003.

14. Mannion, p. 8.

15. Jennifer Ragland, "Stores' Tobacco Ads Targeting Children," *The Los Angeles Times*, April 24, 2001.

16. Ibid.

17. Ibid.

18. Ibid.

19. Gordon Fairclough, "Study Slams Philip Morris Ads Telling Teens Not to Smoke," *The Wall Street Journal*, May 29, 2002.

20. Ibid.

21. Ibid.

22. "Higher Cigarette Taxes Deter Teen Smokers," *The Los Angeles Times*, May 25, 2002.

23. Ibid.

24. Ibid.

25. Reuters, "Report Shows Slight Decline in U.S. Teen Smoking," April 2, 2002.

26. Murphy.

27. Mannion, p. 61.

Chapter 6.   Eating Disorders: Deadly Behavior

1. Sharlene Hesse-Biber, *Am I Thin Enough Yet?* (New York: Oxford University Press, 1996), p. 82.

2. Olive Barker, "Prevention of Anorexia Has to Start Young," *USA Today*, October 19, 1999.

3. Ibid.

4. Hesse-Biber, p. 28.

5. Ibid., p. 121.

6. Ibid., p. 101.

7. Nina Barraclough, "More Obese Teens Opting for Weight-Loss Surgery," *Miami Herald*, November 2003.

8. Ibid.

9. Hesse-Biber, p. 83.

10. Ibid.

11. Cherry Boone O'Neill, *Starving For Attention* (Center City, Minn.: Hazelden, 1992), p. 52.

12. Emily Wax, "Immigrant Girls Are Starving to Be American," *The Washington Post*, March 6, 2000.

13. Ibid.

14. Ibid.

15. Eleena de Lisser, "A Radical New Approach to Anorexia," *The Wall Street Journal*, August 21, 2002, p. D1.

16. Rose Marie Feagin, "Eating Disorders on the Rise," *The Mansfield (Ohio) News Journal*, August 18, 2003.

17. Erica Goode, "Thinner: The Male Battle With Anorexia," *The New York Times*, June 25, 2000.

18. Ibid.

19. Ibid.

20. Marlene Boskin-White and William C. White, Jr., *Bulimia/Anorexia: The Binge-Purge Cycle and Self-Starvation* (New York: W.W. Norton and Company, 2000), p. 111.

21. Ibid., p. 114.

22. Ibid., p. 117.

23. Ibid., p. 124.

24. Feagin.

25. Barker.

26. de Lisser.

Chapter 7.   Self-Mutilation: A Cry for Help

1. Michele Mandel, "Wounds Run Deep," *The Toronto Sun*, September 22, 2002.

2. Ibid.

3. Ibid.

4. Ibid.

5. Ibid.

6. Nancy Walsh, "Self-cutting Is Almost Epidemic in Adolescents," *Pediatric News*, September 2002.

7. Steven Levenkron, *Cutting: Understanding and Overcoming Self-Mutilation* (New York: W.W. Norton and Company, 1998), p. 24.

8. Walsh.

9. Marilee Strong, *A Bright Red Scream, Self-mutilation and the Language of Pain* (New York: Viking, 1998), p. 18.

10. Martha Irvine, "Self-Mutilation Syndrome Also Scars Victims' Self-Image," *The Los Angeles Times*, March 10, 2002.

11. Batya Swift Yasgur, "Antisuicidal Effect of Self-Injury Calls for Tolerance," *Clinical Psychiatry News*, July 2001, p. 50.

12. Strong, p. 59.

13. Levenkron, p. 105.

14. Ibid., p. 111.

15. Ibid., p. 44.

16. Irvine.

17. Ibid.

18. Ibid.

19. Strong, p. 3.

20. Ibid.

21. Ibid., p. 187.

22. Ibid., p. 193.

23. Yasgur.

24. Ibid.

25. Ibid.

26. Ibid.

Chapter 8.   The Internet: Obsession and Isolation

1. CyberAtlas staff, "U.S. Internet Population Continues to Grow," n.d., <www.ask.com> (December 21, 2002).

2. Peter Mitchell, "Internet Addiction: Genuine Diagnosis or Not?" *The Lancet*, February 19, 2000, p. 632.

3. Ibid.

4. Susan Gast, "Addiction to Internet Use Can Come in Several Forms," *The Atlanta Journal*, September 9, 2001.

5. Ibid.

6. Ibid.

7. Alex Hall and Jeffrey Parsons, "Internet Addiction: College Student Case Study Using Best Practices in Cognitive Behavior Therapy," *Journal of Mental Health Counseling*, October 2001, p. 312.

8. Bill Biggar and Joe Myers, *Danger Zones: What Parents Should Know About the Internet* (Kansas City, Mo.: Andrews and McMeel, 1996), p. 30.

9. Gloria Goodale, "Parents Out of E-loop," *The Christian Science Monitor*, September 20, 2001.

10. Ibid.

11. Ibid.

12. "See No Evil: How Internet Filters Affect the Search for On-line Health Information," December 10, 2002, <http://www.kff.org/entmedia/3294-index.cfm> (July 27, 2005).

13. Arian Campo-Flores, "A Chat-Room Encounter's Tragic End," *Newsweek*, June 3, 2002.

14. Ibid.

15. Ariana Eunjung Cha, "Dear Web Diary, SO Much to Tell!!" *The Washington Post*, September 2, 2001.

16. Ibid.

17. Ibid.

18. Ibid.

19. Daniel Yi, "Orange County; At Cyber Cafes, Playing Games Can Turn Serious," *The Los Angeles Times,* June 16, 2002.

20. Ibid.

21. Ibid.

22. Michael Janofsky, "Youth Pleads An Addiction to the Internet in Threat Case," *The New York Times,* January 13, 2000.

23. Ibid.

24. Ibid.

25. Harmon Leon, "Bizarre Legal Defenses," *CriminalDefense Weekly,* April 15–21, 2002, <http://www.criminaldefense.com> (October 2003).

26. Biggar and Myers, p. 97.

27. "Are You Becoming an Internet Addict?" *USA Today,* May 2001, p. 7.

28. Pamela LiCalzi O'Connell, "On-line Diary," *The New York Times,* January 3, 2002.

29. Carolyn Jabs, "Addicted to the Net," *FamilyPC,* March 2001, p. 72.

30. Sharon Gaudin "Facebook Use Linked to Teen Psych Disorders," *Computerworld,* August 8, 2011, <http://www.computerworld.com/s/article/print/9218991/Facebook_use_linked_to_teen_psych_disorders?taxonomyName=Web+Apps&taxonomyId=169> (October 20, 2012).

31. Caharine Paddock PhD. "Facebook Addiction – New Psychological Scale," *Medical News Today,* May 11, 2012, <http://www.medicalnewstoday.com/articles/245251.php> (October 20,2012).

32. Stefan Kiesbye, ed. *Distracted Driving.* (New York: Greenhaven Press, 2012). p. 16.

33. Stefan Kiesbye, ed. *Cell Phones and Driving.* (New York: Greenhaven Press, 2011). p.63.

34. Genevra Pittman, "Sexting Again Linked to Risky Sex Among Teens," *Montreal Gazette,* September 17, 2012, <http://www.montrealgazette.com/story_print.html?id=7253068&sponsor=> (October 20, 2012).

35. Deborah Feyerick and Sheila Steffen, "Sexting Lands Teen on Offender List," *CNN.com*, 2008, <http://www.cnn.com/2009/CRIME/04/07/sexting.busts/index.html > (October 20, 2012).

36. Mike Celizic, "Her Teen Committed Suicide Over Texting," *NBCNEWS.com*, <http://www.cnn.com/2009/CRIME/04/07/sexting.busts/index.html> (October 20, 2012).

37. Ibid.

Chapter 9.   What Can Help

1. Tara Parker-Pope, "Helping Kids Deal With Stresses of Life May Be Most Effective Antidrug Strategy," *The Wall Street Journal*, May 21, 2002.

2. Ibid.

3. Genaro C. Armas, "The 2000 Census: Number of One-Parent Families Increases Worldwide," *The Associated Press*, Washington, D.C., November 21, 2001.

4. Marlene Cimons, "What Gets Teens in Trouble," *The Los Angeles Times*, December 1, 2000.

5. Ibid.

6. Francine Kiefer, "Teenagers Want More . . . Family Time?" *The Christian Science Monitor*, May 3, 2000.

7. Ibid.

8. Linda Marsa, "Substance Abuse: Family Life Cushions Teens Against Trouble," *The Los Angeles Times*, August 6, 2001.

9. Caroline M. Levchuck, Jane Kelly Kosek, and Michele Drohan, "Habits and Behaviors," *Healthy Living*, 2000.

Glossary

addiction—A compulsive need to do something regardless of consequences.

anorexia—An eating disorder in which someone severely limits his or her food intake.

bath salts—White powder that contains chemicals which provide a high with severe hallucinations.

bulimia—An eating disorder in which someone eats a large amount, then purges the food.

chat room—On-line service where members communicate by typing messages to each other in real time.

compulsive—Unable to control an action.

dehydration—A potentially dangerous condition in which the body is depleted of water.

diuretic—A drug that causes an increase in the amount of urine the kidneys produce.

dopamine—A neurotransmitter in the brain's limbic system, a section associated with feelings of pleasure.

ecstasy—A relatively inexpensive, trendy "designer" drug.

endorphins—Natural hormones in the body that can alter mood and relieve pain.

ephedra—A weight-loss drug that can cause rapid heartbeat and has been associated with some deaths.

Facebook—A free social networking website that allows members to create profiles, send and receive messages.

Freon (CFC, chlorofluorocarbon)—A gas used as a refrigerant and as a propellant for aerosols.

gateway drug—A drug that serves as an introduction to stronger, more harmful drugs.

huffing—Soaking a rag with an inhalant and putting it over the nose and mouth and inhaling; also, a slang term for all types of inhaling.

laxative—A substance that brings on a bowel movement.

neurological—Pertaining to the nerves and the nervous system, particularly in reference to diseases of either.

nicotine—A highly toxic, addictive ingredient found in all tobacco products.

psychologist—Someone who specializes in the study of the mind and behavior.

puberty—Preteen or early teen years during which the body changes and becomes able to reproduce.

purge—To rid the body of food, usually through vomiting, laxatives, diuretics, or exercise.

rehabilitation—The process of restoring someone to good health.

Social media—Internet based applications that allow users to keep in touch through their computers or cell phones.

sexting—Sending sexually explicit messages or images by use of cell phone or other mobile device.

steroid—A hormone that promotes the synthesis of proteins and the building of muscle mass (also called anabolic or anabolic-androgenic steroid).

texting—Brief written messages sent through a cell phone or similar mobile device.

virtual—The effect of seeming to be real, such as in computer-generated special effects often seen in movies and computer games.

For More Information

Alateen
P.O. Box 862 Midtown Station
New York, N.Y. 10018-0862
1-800-344-2666
212-302-7240

American Anorexia/ Bulimia Association
165 West 46th St. #1108
New York, N.Y. 10036
212-575-6200

Hazelden Foundation
P.O. Box 11
Center City, Minn. 55012-0011
1-800-257-7810

National Eating Disorders
603 Stewart St., Suite 803
Seattle, Wash. 98101
206-382-3587

National Inhalant Prevention Coalition
2904 Kerby Ln.
Austin, Tex. 78703
1-800-269-4237
512-480-8953

National Institute on Drug Abuse
6001 Executive Blvd.
Rockville, Md. 20852
301-443-6245

The Partnership for a Drug-Free America
405 Lexington Ave., Suite 1601
New York, N.Y. 10174
212-922-1560

SAFE
(Self-Abuse Finally Ends)
40 Timberline Dr.
Lemont, Ill. 60439
1-800-DONTCUT

Further Reading

Bjonlund, Lydia. *Alcohol*. North Mankato Minn.: Cherry Lake Publishing, 2008.

Greene, Jessica R. *Eating Disorders: The Ultimate Teen Guide.* Manham, Maryland: Rowman & Littlefield Publishers, 2014.

Kuhn, Cynthia, Scott Swartzwelder, Wilkie Wilson and Jeremy Foster. *Buzzed: The Straight Facts About the Most Used and Abused Drugs from Alcohol to Ecstasy.* New York: W.W. Norton & Company, 2014.

Laser, Tammy and Stephanie Watson. *Eating Disorders.* New York: Rosen Publishing, Inc., 2011.

Miller, Heather. *Smoking.* North Mankato Minn.: Cherry Lake Publishing, 2008.

Walker, Ida. *Addiction Treatment: Escaping the Trap.* Broomall Penn.: Mason Crest Publishers, 2012.

Internet Addresses

National Eating Disorders

<http://www.nationaleatingdisorders.org>

National Institute on Drug Abuse

<http://www.drugabuse.gov>

Teen Issues

<http://www.teenhelp.com>

Index